Nowhere Near
The Middle

The Life Story of Valerie Doshier

Written by

Keith E. Smith
with
D'Ann Swain

Dream In Magic Publishing

ISBN: 978-1-7352093-1-9

Cover Design:
Laura Ramsey
Cameron Ramsey

Cover photo by
Jennifer Marez

Preface

A writer typically writes the book they want to write. It might be a work of their imagination, something they're passionate about, or a book intended to educate. However, some books demand to be written. Not in a forceful way, but in a way where the story relentlessly haunts an author until they are compelled to write it.

That's how this book came to be.

It was the summer of 2019, and I'd been traveling with a group of writers. We were on our way back from Colorado where we had spent nearly two months writing while staying in a Rocky Mountain cabin. We had to find a place to stop for the night, so one of my companions booked an Airbnb for us in the Texas Panhandle town of Vega. None of us had heard of Vega before and didn't know what to expect.

We arrived at night, and though we couldn't tell much about the town in the dark, it seemed like a pleasant enough place. It had escaped our attention when we booked our accommodations that we would be staying on Route 66, but some brochures in our room clued us in. We were exhausted and decided we'd take a look around the next day.

The next morning, a friend and I left the Airbnb to do a little exploring before we left town. We crossed the street to look at the Oldham County Courthouse. From there, we spotted the historic Magnolia Service Station down the street, a relic of the heydays of the historic Mother Road.

While we were checking out the restored station, something across the street caught my eye. It was a beautiful mural painted on the side of an old building. I was drawn to it, so we crossed the street for a closer look. It was a beautiful piece of artwork depicting Comancheros trading with the Comanche people, and reflected the history of the area. We walked around to the front of the building and discovered that it was actually the Milburn-Price Culture Museum. The museum was filled with a treasure trove of artifacts, all relating to the history of the area. Karen Conn, one of the museum's curators, greeted us on the porch and invited us inside for a look around. Karen seemed to know all the details about every item on display, and was the perfect guide for our journey back in time.

However, the highlight of the tour occurred when she took us to a second building situated just behind the main part of the museum. The second building was a work in progress, where several upcoming displays were underway. We were standing outside the entrance to the building when Karen paused and told us that inside we would see a mural on one of the walls, which was a tribute to a young woman named Valerie Doshier. She gave us an abbreviated version of Valerie's story, and it was easy to see that the story was deeply meaningful to Karen.

In that moment, everything I had been feeling up to that point changed. Before, I was simply a happy traveler who was passing through an interesting, small town in Texas. I was enjoying the experience, one of many that summer, and would soon be on my way to my next destination. While Karen was telling us the story, I was inexplicably drawn to every word. I wanted to know more. I *had* to know more.

We stepped inside and our hostess showed us several displays that were under construction. It was all interesting, but when I turned a corner and laid my eyes on the tribute mural, I froze. The mural had been painted by Joshua Finley, a dear friend of Valerie's, and it was a repre-sensation of a conversation that Valerie had with her mother about infinity (you'll read about that conversation later in this book). Something about the energy of this mural pierced my heart. Everything else faded into the background, and I wanted to sit and hear everything I possibly could about the young woman depicted on the mural before me. I'd never experienced anything like that before, and I didn't know what was happening inside of me. It caught me completely by surprise. Why was I affected so deeply? Why did I feel the intense desire to know more? Of all the things I'd experienced that year, why did that moment hit me so hard? I didn't have answers to any of the questions swirling through my mind.

After our tour was complete, and following a ride around town in a Humvee—courtesy of Karen's husband, Greg Conn—we headed back to our Airbnb and prepared to leave. I parted ways with my traveling companions and continued my journey alone. I was headed toward West Texas to visit family, and to see where life would lead me next. The trip was about five hours, and the entire way I couldn't shake the feeling that had come over me in the museum. I reached my destination and got lost in a myriad of activities, and the intense feelings subsided.

It was about a week later when they all came back. I decided to write a blog post about it and tell the story of my experience passing through Vega. At the time, I felt that would be the end of it, and the experience would simply be archived in my memories. I was wrong.

The blog post set off a flurry of social media comments, messages, and emails from Valerie's friends and family. I was blown away when both of her parents contacted me, thanking me for what I'd written. I was amazed by the response, but it also confirmed that what I'd been feeling was real.

Over the next several months, Valerie's story would come back to me again and again. It wasn't like I was trying to forget about it, I was just a working writer trying to stay busy enough to survive, but I couldn't have forgotten her if I tried. The same feeling that came over me that day in Vega, when I saw her tribute mural on the wall of the museum, visited me more frequently. As time passed, it became clear that there was no escaping the hold Valerie's story had on me. By that time, I was communicating regularly with her mother, who presented me with an intriguing thought: Maybe Valerie chose me to write her story.

I was taken aback by her comment. Me? Why would she choose me? I had never met Valerie, and though I'd written four books, never before had I written anything like that. Admittedly, I doubted that I was the writer for the task. In the end, I surrendered to the feeling that had been driving me for months. I wasn't sure how I was going to do it, but I would write Valerie Doshier's story.

Of course, this book wouldn't have been possible without the help of Valerie's mother, D'Ann Swain. Her unwavering commitment to seeing Valerie's story told is what made this possible. She typed thousands of words, relived months of painful history, and was a tremendous resource.

Like Valerie, this book is unique because it doesn't fit a particular mold. It isn't a true memoir, but it's more than a mere biographical account of Valerie's life. This book is written in the first person, as if Valerie is telling her own story. The idea for that came to me in a peculiar way, and attempting to describe it here would cheapen the experience and come off sounding contrived or artificial. I ran the idea past D'Ann during one of our phone conversations, and she thought we should try it. I wrote a few pages and sent them to her for review, and she loved it. And then the work began.

How do you shrink a life so big and a light so bright to fit nicely within the confines of a few pages?

The answer is simple: You don't.

I could've written a book of epic length, and it still would've fallen short of adequately capturing a life so full of love, freedom, and adventure.

Valerie often said that the only thing that mattered is love, and that's the place from which I have written this book.

Albert Einstein once wrote, "A human being is a part of the whole, called by us 'Universe,' a part limited in time and space. He experiences himself, his thoughts and feelings as something separated from the rest, a kind of optical delusion of his consciousness. This delusion is a kind of prison for us, restricting us to our personal desires and to affection for a few persons nearest to us. Our task must be to free ourselves from this prison by widening our circle of compassion to embrace all living creatures and the whole nature in its beauty."

He went on to say that no one is able to completely achieve the task of freeing themselves from the prison of delusion he mentions in this passage, but I suspect Valerie got closer than most.

Keith E. Smith

Valerie working on the mural for the
Milburn-Price Culture Museum.

Milburn-Price Culture Museum. Mural painted by Joshua
Finley & Valerie Doshier, nearing its completion.

Our Earth Angel

A Poem for Valerie
by Deb Hedges

She came to us an earth angel bearing gifts of love, beauty, grace, courage, and strength. We are mesmerized by her creativity, artistic expression, hopes and dreams—dreams far too great for this meager existence—dreams that only eternity can hold.

She was meant to serve a greater purpose. A purpose beyond our comprehension. Her journey has been to bring these gifts, these blessings, these lessons, this inspiration, to learn and to prepare her spirit to soar.

When her soul is set free the sky will become her canvas. She will paint the stars, the moon, the sun, and the most beautiful rainbows. We will hear her sing in the wind, the rain, the thunder and the silence. We will feel her presence, her love, her beauty and know she has earned her heavenly wings with dignity and grace.

That it is time for her to fly and serve her higher purpose. A purpose far too great for our minds to conceive. A purpose that someday we will comprehend.

Val Wonder is truly one of the most beautiful souls to grace this earth. Prayers for peace, strength, courage, solace, comfort and a beautiful transition for Val Wonder.

Prologue

Most people don't expect to die at thirty.

I know I didn't.

I'd spent my life as a free spirit, an explorer who traveled the world soaking up every ounce of beauty I could find. I'd made friends in other countries, fell in love, and I—

Well, I wasn't finished.

I had murals and canvases to paint. There were still so many places in the world I hadn't seen, people I hadn't met, and songs I hadn't written. More than anything, I was in love and there was a beautiful future waiting for me. Yet, there I was in a hospital emergency room with a doctor telling me otherwise.

I thought that it must've been a mistake. But it wasn't a mistake. It was cancer. Grade 4 glioblastoma, the worst possible kind.

What are you supposed to do when you receive that kind of news? Your life is moving along, you're chasing dreams, and then all of a sudden, somebody slams on the brakes. You didn't choose it. You didn't want it. But then, no one asked if you did. It just happened.

I can't imagine how Mom felt. She had been a neuro nurse for years, and was the first person the doctor told about the large tumor in my brain after reviewing the results of the MRI.

It must have crushed her, but she tried to put on a brave face when she walked into the room and said, "Honey, I have bad news. There's a tumor in your brain, and it's big."

That's how it was with us. Mom and I didn't sugarcoat truth, and she knew I'd want her to give it to me straight. Mom was a nurse and she fully understood the weight her words carried.

All I could do was cry and refuse to accept that it was true. Doctors and nurses, most of whom had worked with Mom, poured into the room. I knew they were trying to make me feel better, but I was in shock. I needed time to think and to process what was happening to me.

After everyone left, Mom crawled into my bed. We cried and talked, trying to wrap our heads around it all. I wish I could explain the deluge of thoughts and feelings I experienced in those moments, but it was just too much.

In the midst of that river of emotion, one thought rose to the surface.

This is not about me.

Yes, I was the one who had been diagnosed with a brain tumor that would take my life, but that was just one piece of a larger picture. It was not unlike one of my paintings. You could focus on one minuscule area of the canvas and think that's all there is, but if you widen your perspective, you can take in the beauty of the whole thing. I knew it was time to widen my perspective about what was happening to me. The deadly brain tumor was only a small part of something bigger.

It may seem odd that I would think like that, but it wasn't something new for me. All of my life I had been taught to think of others and have compassion for those in need. As a child, my mom would drive me around the poorer neighborhoods of Amarillo, Texas and show me what poverty looked like. My grandmother had done the same for my mom, and would tell her, "See all of this? This is not right. These people have nothing. We must take care of them."

I knew my ordeal would bring pain to many people, especially those close to me. I couldn't stop that from happening, but I could use my situation to inspire others to live their life full on. Maybe I could help them not fear death too. It wasn't going to be easy, but I had to try. I was devastated and scared, but I was determined to be like a rock cast into a pond, from which ripples would travel outward to the very edges. The rock may sink to the bottom, but the ripples go on.

"Mom, you know our job in all of this is to be an inspiration to others."

I spoke those words to my mother as we laid in bed crying. It hurt to see the tears in her eyes, but she knew I was right. In the coming months, I would lean on Mom more and more, but thanks to her, my family, friends, and my beloved Nathan, I became that rock.

And now, the ripples have reached you.

Valerie & Travis

Part 1

Val Wonder

When you've been told your life could end in a matter of months, you start doing some serious reflecting. How did I get to that place in time? What in my life had shaped me into the person I'd become? Was my life meaningful? How did my upbringing influence me? Why was I born into my specific family? The questions are endless.

For me, my life was about exploration. Not the kind of exploring where I traveled to distant lands, though that was part of it, but an exploration of what it meant to be *alive* and to live from my heart.

When I look back, I can see a common thread that was woven throughout my life. It's a thread that reaches all the way back to my childhood and weaves itself into a kind of theme. That theme was a loving, unbridled passion for life that became the canvas upon which the colors of my life were displayed.

I was born in the Texas Panhandle, where the land is flat and the sky is big. Surrounded by all that open space and a never-ending sky, it's no wonder I grew up with the view that life was full of endless possibilities. I was never satisfied with sitting on the sidelines of life. I had to be hands-on, involved, and experience everything for myself.

There was little I wouldn't try if given half a chance. Why? Because, even as a child, I was in love with living. I'm sure my zeal was a lot for my parents to handle at times, but I'm grateful I was allowed to be me.

My enthusiasm for life showed itself at an early age. Because of vision issues, I had to start wearing bifocals before I was one year old. By the age of three, I was picking out my own frames, which always had to be pink. This is why, years later, the childrens' book character I would create (Cheeky MaNeeky) always wore pink glasses.

Kids grow fast and my parents had to buy me new glasses about every six months. Of course, there were a few "accidents" along the way that required them to be replaced as well. Once, when I was about three years old, my older brother Travis and I were playing in some mud in our front yard. My lenses got so dirty I couldn't see. Being a good brother, Travis tried to clean them for me, only he did so by using the concrete sidewalk to scrape the mud from the lenses. Needless to say, we had to make a trip back to the optometrist and get new lenses.

I love telling that story because it shows how Travis always looked out for me, even if cleaning my glasses on the sidewalk wasn't the greatest idea. When we were little, Mom used to tell us that it was important for us to like each other. If we didn't, then the friends each of us made as we grew up wouldn't like each other either, and Travis and I would grow apart. It's sad to think of how often siblings are conditioned to believe they're not supposed to get along, much less be best friends.

Oh, don't get me wrong. Like most siblings, Travis and I had our share of disagreements. For instance, there was the time we were helping our ranch foreman, Toby, work cattle and clean out a stock tank. We were still in high school then, and though we got along wonderfully most of the time, on that day we clashed. I was hot, tired, and not happy about the work we were doing. Travis kept teasing me, and I guess I reached a point where I'd had enough. We ended up in a physical fight, which consisted of him holding me back and laughing. Of course, that didn't improve my mood one bit. He kept telling me to calm down which, as you might imagine, had no calming effect on me whatsoever.

Toby finally broke us up, and for years he loved to tell that story every chance he got. I guess you could say I never had a problem sticking up for myself. Aside from the occasional skirmish, Travis and I developed a bond that went beyond being brother and sister. We became best friends too. He was my voice of reason, and anytime I'd want to run headlong into some wild idea, he was there to talk me off the cliff. I loved him for that. I guess we must've taken Mom's advice to heart because we were always close, and grew up with the same group of friends.

You might have the impression that I was a bit headstrong, and you'd be right. Being a strong-willed child, you can bet I got myself into trouble quite a bit. I'm sure I drove my parents crazy at times, but I never once doubted that I was deeply loved. I'm not sure how they were able to pull that off, but I'm so grateful they did.

I can't explain where or how I got the insight at such a young age, but when I was about four or five years old, I stopped misbehaving. It was like someone flipped a switch. Naturally, my mother was more than a little surprised, and asked me what had changed. I explained to her that I had gotten tired of being bad and getting into trouble all the time. From that time forward, I was more pleasant. I had been told on more than one occasion that I was an "old soul," and maybe that's where flashes of wisdom like that came from. Maybe, but who knows? I'm sure Mom didn't know what to make of it, but I suspect she was thankful nonetheless.

Above: Cheeky MaNeeky
Below: Valerie

Even as a child, my zeal for life was apparent. Since I had the tendency to make every experience a thrilling one, I was seldom bored. I remember often encouraging my friends to "take a dare" with me. I lived life as though it were a grand adventure, and wanted everyone to come along with me for the joyous ride. Living life like that is addicting, but in only the best ways.

When I was little, my grandmother made superhero capes for all her grandkids. I would run through the house with the cape flowing behind me as if I was about to take flight. My Uncle Mike started calling me Val Wonder. A fitting nickname I think, and one that stuck with me for the rest of my life. It wasn't an alter ego as much as it was an extension of my personality. It was a kind of description of my disposition or character.

As a little girl, I was never too interested in girly stuff. Barbie dolls weren't my thing, but I did, however, love chocolate. I used to wear a clip-on button on my jacket that read, "I Love Chocolate." What I was into was playing outside and doing whatever Travis was doing. When he wasn't around, I usually had my friend Sarah over.

Unlike my big brother, Sarah wasn't the voice of reason and we'd often pull off some escapades that got us into trouble. Once, we thought it would be a grand idea to get creative with paints and paper. Well, merely painting with brushes wasn't good enough for us, so we took off our shoes, stepped in the paint and then onto the paper. Not satisfied with that, we took it up a notch and began jumping off the couch onto the paper—and carpet—with our paint-soaked feet. That experiment, as you might've guessed, didn't turn out so well for either of us.

Growing up, I spent a lot of time with family and friends. I really enjoyed all the mischief we'd get into on overnight visits. I was often the first one to drink whatever experimental concoction we kids came up with, or the ready and willing volunteer to jump off the tallest piece of farm equipment in the barn. I even convinced my brother, who was usually the voice of reason, to pull our trampoline close to the house so we could jump onto it from the roof of our house. I tried to help people be brave and live life fully like it was my job.

Sometimes, things didn't go as planned. Like the time I talked my friend Kris into touching a skunk we'd found in the water well box. That little adventure ended with her crying in the bathtub as our moms poured tomato juice over her to get the smell off. Yet another adventure I filed under, "It seemed like a good idea at the time." Val Wonder strikes again.

Then there was the time Travis and I were staying with my mom's cousin Robin and her husband Shane. Robin made us supper that night, and as usual, Travis and I took a long time to eat. Meals were always a social event for us, and we never rushed them. Supper included peas, and Robin told us that we couldn't get down from the table until we had eaten our peas. Robin and Shane left the room, and that's the moment a light bulb went on in my head. Rather than eat the disgusting peas, I decided that we could secretly smash them into the middle crack of the table. Travis was a little hesitant, but I coaxed him into doing it, and when the job was complete, we got up and never said a word. Robin called me out on that years later. It seems I was an "outside the box" thinker at an early age.

My family was especially important to me. I loved my parents, grandparents, and cousins, and always took comfort in knowing they loved me back. Anytime my family was piled on the couch, you'd find me sitting in the center, right in the middle of all that love. There were four of us in the cousin crew: Travis, me, Hillary, and her little brother Joel. We were all about two years apart in age. Hillary was a girly girl, but I loved her so much. She would have all her dolls set up in her room for a tea party, and Joel and I would crash in and tear it all up. I admit that it was I who talked Joel into those terrorizing adventures of fun, which later ended with us getting in trouble. My apologies, Joel.

Speaking of Joel, I still don't know how he survived our childhood. We spent a lot of time playing together at our grandparent's house. They had a huge yard at the front and back of their place, and we enjoyed a lot of independence when we played there. We'd put Joel in our red wagon and push him down the sidewalk as fast as we could. He'd have to use the handle of the wagon to steer himself into the grass so he wouldn't careen out into the very busy street. Probably not the safest of childhood games, but I would cheer him on and let him know how special he was.

We all had active imaginations and boy did we come up with some weird games at my grandparents' house. I remember how we'd gather up crab apples, dump them into an old black cauldron in the backyard, add some water, and make "soup." Then there was the game we called "spider jumping," where we'd climb up onto the brick fence and jump off. Now that I think about it, it seems like most of our games involved an element of danger for some reason. I'm sure my family would say that, more often than not, I was that reason.

When Travis started school, a full year before me, I was lost. I missed him so much. Mom was fun, but not like Travis. I was bored without him around, and that forced me to make up my own adventures. One day, the post office called and said we had received a shipment of baby chicks, so Mom and I climbed into our car and drove to town. The chicks came in a cardboard box, and when we got back home, Mom let me carry the box inside. I carefully set them down on the dining room floor.

Mom cautioned me, "Valerie don't open that box. If you do, they will jump out and be everywhere. Travis will be home soon and we will take them to the barn."

I said, "Okay," but got excited while peeking at the chicks through holes in the box.

Mom was busy in the kitchen and couldn't see what was about to happen. I slowly reached over, grabbed the lid, and opened the box. Just as Mom predicted, baby chicks began to jump out and spread out all over the house. I was laughing with excitement. Hearing my laughter, Mom knew something was up and rushed back into the dining room. The baby chicks were running in every direction, and I howled with laughter as she chased them through the house.

The following year, I was finally old enough to start school. I loved it! New fun, new friends, and even more adventures! I was taught to be kind to other kids, no matter who they were or what they looked like. After all, I didn't like it when some kids would call me four-eyes.

I tried my best at the kindness and compassion thing. Travis was kind to everyone and had lots of friends, so it was easy to follow his lead. I was young, and already wanted everyone to be happy and like themselves for who they were. I strove to be nice to all kids and make them laugh if I could. I'm sure some people thought I was just being silly, but I somehow knew that if I could make a person laugh they would be happier.

Valerie's childhood home.

I would even make fun of myself if that's what it took, and doing so had a way of making others more comfortable with themselves. My pink glasses had thick bifocal lenses. I would take them off, hold them next to my face, and move them back and forth in front of one eye, which caused my eye to be supersized. We called that the "big eye." It made everyone laugh, and showed others that wearing glasses was super cool.

I grew up on a ranch in Texas, and was taught to love and respect animals in the same way as human beings. We had chickens, cattle, horses, and even a few pigs. Travis and I would also catch birds, snakes, lizards, mice, and more. You name it, we probably caught it and took care of it at some point. Travis was always the patient one when it came to catching varmints, and we had some exciting adventures. Truth be told, we may or may not have lost the occasional hermit crab and snake in the house, which kept things interesting for sure. I guess the point is that whether it was humans or animals, love just made things better. Life is hard enough as it is, but love has a way of smoothing out the rough spots.

Mom and Dad instilled a strong work ethic in Travis and me, and life on a farm helped them do that. They expected us to do all kinds of chores. We even helped with the cattle. One day when I was about seven years old, I remember that Dad was going back to check on the cattle. It was winter and they were feeding on winter wheat. He always drove his old flatbed Ford when he went to check on them, and I asked to go with him. Dad knew how much I loved being outdoors and working on the farm. He said yes, and off we went.

We had to stop several times to open and close gates as we drove through the various pastures. After about the third time of stopping to open and close a gate, Dad asked if I wanted to drive the truck through the next gate after he opened it. Of course I said yes, with a huge smile and eyebrows raised in excitement. He gave me a quick tutorial, explaining how to use the accelerator and brakes, and that I should keep both hands on the steering wheel. He later told me that when he went to open the gate and turned back to look at me, all he could see was me looking at him between the steering wheel and dashboard as I gunned the truck through the gate, eyes wide open—a kind of metaphor for how I would live my whole life.

One of our chores at home was mowing the yard every week. I never wanted to mow the north side, and would talk Travis or Mom into doing it. It wasn't until years later when I explained why. I didn't want to mow the side yard because there was always a lady there who was wearing a flowing white dress and floating among trees. I often wondered why nobody else ever saw her. It's hard to say why I kept that information to myself for all those years, but I think seeing that "lady" in the trees sparked my spiritual curiosity.

We went to church regularly, and I had lots of friends there. In fact, I discovered my love for singing in church. Music fed my soul, even as a child, and continued to play an important role throughout my life. I was so excited about singing in those days that I wrote a letter to Whitney Houston. She never wrote back, but I didn't care. I kept on singing.

As the years went on, my focus shifted and I became involved in running track. I could outrun everyone my age and I especially enjoyed outrunning the boys. It was fun to prove that girls were just as capable, even if some people had a hard time accepting that fact.

Valerie & Travis

The track meets at the end of the school year were some of my favorite events. By the time I reached junior high, I was laser-focused on athletics and cheerleading. I loved the thrill and fast pace of it all, especially track. I wanted to be a track star, and dedicated all my spare time to perfecting my craft with a coach. When my friends were at the swimming pool, or just hanging out, I was taking track lessons from a private coach. Mom and I traveled to track meets all over the state. All the hard work paid off because I qualified for the National Hershey track meet in Pennsylvania and the Junior Olympics in Charlotte, North Carolina. I had to pick just one of these and my choice was the Junior Olympics.

Mom and I flew to Charlotte. When we arrived, we saw kids from all over, many with their coaches and fancy two-way radios. All I had was myself and my mom, and I wasn't the least bit intimidated. I just wanted to compete. I qualified for the finals in two events, but what I remember most about that trip was being intrigued with a part of the world I had never seen before.

Mom wanted to go sightseeing in the historic district, and I wanted to see the poverty-stricken part of town. I wanted to witness firsthand what it was like there. So, Mom took me to the parts of Charlotte that others often avoided. It was plain to see the intense need of the people there, and the impression it made upon me was deep. It fueled the fires of my compassion. I knew there was enough in the world for everyone, yet wondered why there were so many who had almost nothing. I wanted to help lighten their burden somehow and give them what they needed, especially love.

Like I said earlier, facing your own mortality causes you to take a closer look at your life. As sad as it is, knowing death is near brings a sense of clarity that is nearly impossible to obtain in any other way. It strips away any pretense or preconceived notions about what it means to be alive. It also gives you a deep appreciation for the people in your life and the amazing things you've experienced. If I had to pick just one thing that shaped me into the kind of person I was, it would probably be my love for people. I never much cared about where a person was from, what they'd done wrong in the past, the color of their skin, or their level of education. I loved people right where they were, and hoped they'd do the same for me in return.

Of course, all of that was rooted in my upbringing. It began with the encouragement I was given to love my big brother, cousins, and others in my family, and it branched out from there. I remember the times Mom would drive me and my brother through the poor neighborhoods of Amarillo, Texas. She would talk to us about the homeless, their suffering, and how those people were just like us, only they had more challenges. She told us that her mom had done the same with her when she was growing up. Lessons like that made a lasting impression on both me and Travis. So much so, that we put the lessons we learned into action.

Like many kids growing up in the rural areas of the Texas Panhandle, we rode a bus to school. There were a couple of kids we rode the bus with who weren't as fortunate as us. They seemed to always be shy and a little sad. Travis and I talked to them often on our bus rides and found out that they weren't eating at home. They were hungry, and it was mind-blowing to us because we couldn't imagine what that was like. We enjoyed home-cooked meals, and healthy snacks were always waiting for us when we got home from school. Their situation was heart-breaking and we decided to do something about it.

Travis and I started to sneak extra food from the "snack basket" at our house for our friends on the bus. That plan worked great, but I felt we needed to do even more, so I started taking packages of crackers from the cafeteria at school. A lot of packages. My second grade teacher must have seen me and called Mom. She told her I had been stealing crackers from the cafeteria and couldn't imagine why. When we got home from school that day, Mom asked us about it. We looked at each other, thinking we were in trouble, and came clean. Instead of Mom getting mad, she let us know she was proud of us for caring about those kids. Mom ended up visiting their home and was able to get them the help they needed. Mom told us that what we did was, "Love in action."

I never forgot that. Love is so much more than feelings and emotions. It is those things, but love is also a verb. If you love someone, you'll demonstrate that love through your actions. Love is alive. It's movement and action, and is never dormant.

I learned a lot about life through observation. Even as a young child, I understood the importance of watching and paying attention to other people. As a kid, I insisted that Mom watch everything I was doing. It was important to me.

Living on a ranch kept Mom very busy, especially in the kitchen. She cooked meals for our family of four every day, as well as for several cowboys when we were working cattle. She often tried to get me to stay with her in the kitchen, perhaps hoping I'd pick up some of her culinary skills, but since cooking wasn't on the top of my favorite things to do list, I usually ended up wandering off. I'd venture back to the kitchen every now and then, but it was usually to get Mom to watch me do something I thought was cool. She'd be working hard preparing a meal, and I would burst into the room and exclaim, "Mom! Watch this!"

She'd respond with, "Yes, I see that," as she kept on working.

Naturally, I couldn't let that pass and would say, "No, Mom! Look with your eyes!"

Poor Mom. I knew there was something meaningful about "seeing" someone. Giving them your undivided attention. Years later, Mom would tell me that I taught her the importance of being present in the moment, especially when spending time with others. I'm grateful to have had that understanding at such a young age, and it never left me. I became so good at staying in the moment that others were drawn to me. People often told me that I made them feel important. The truth is, I did consider other people important, and knew the best way to demonstrate that was to pay attention and live in the present. How can you begin to love and care about others if you don't take time to really listen and try to understand them?

I suppose my reputation as a crazy, fun-loving girl goes way back, but I could laser-focus when I was passionate about something. As I mentioned earlier, when I was in junior high I was focused on track and running. By the time I was in my final year, two different colleges had already contacted my private track coach and expressed interest in me. I would start high school the following year. Life was good in those days, and I loved every minute. I was on the basketball team, involved in track, and had a ton of friends.

I remember how Mom would frequently caution me to be careful. I was a wild child, free-spirited and daring. After all, I *was* Val Wonder. She knew it, and reminded me that if I got injured in some way, I may not be able to compete in sports any longer. "Remember your passion," she would say.

I understood what she was trying to do. She didn't want me to take unnecessary risks while riding my horse, playing basketball, or whatever else I was doing. She knew me well, and cautioned me all the time. Frankly, I got tired of hearing it and would roll my eyes every time she said something about it.

Chalk it up to me being a typical teenager, or a bit too much of a "wild child," but I should have paid more attention to her advice. I was at the peak of my athletic abilities and excelled in any sport I was involved in. I remember playing in a basketball tournament during the final game of the competition. I had a great game, and after it was over a lady I didn't know came up to me and said, "You don't know me, and I'm not from here or your hometown, but I drove here today just to watch you play. You're a real go-getter!"

What an amazing compliment. I felt as though I had the world by the tail.

That very day, I went to a friend's house to hang out after the game. It had snowed and we decided to ride four-wheelers. What could go wrong? Well, I had a bad wreck in the snow. I'm not sure how it happened, but I must have attempted some kind of stunt that went wrong.

My parents were called and Dad came and picked me up. By the time I got home, my left knee was swollen and painful. I couldn't put any weight on it. I was upset and scared that I wouldn't be able to play sports for a while.

Mom, being a nurse, looked at my knee and thought it was bad. She also gave me a lecture about not being careful. I didn't roll my eyes that time. The next day, we went to the sports medicine clinic in Amarillo. This was the beginning of a nightmare. I had torn my ACL and crushed my knee, and like a never-ending bad dream, I spent the next two years in rehab. I had two major transplant surgeries, made at least twenty trips to the surgeon to have my knee drained, and endured countless hours of excruciating physical therapy.

Through it all, I was determined to fight my way back into the world of sports I loved so much. Despite all of my efforts, it was not to be. Every time I tried to run or play basketball, even with a full brace on my knee, it would swell, stiffen up, and become so painful I could hardly walk. After several months of anger, frustration, and tears, I finally faced the fact that I wasn't going to play sports again. I was lost. All of my friends were in sports. I still had cheerleading, but my love was sports.

Mom knew I was devastated, and continually encouraged me. She knew I would sink into depression if I didn't shift my focus to something else. She told me that just because I couldn't play sports didn't mean my life wasn't going to be wonderfully successful. She'd say, "It's up to you to change your life, attitude, and focus. You can either feel sorry for yourself and grow bitter, or look at this as an opportunity to shift your focus to another goal. Life is what you make it. God has a plan for you."

Much like her lectures on caution, I grew tired of hearing that I needed to focus my passion in other directions. But unlike previous lectures, this one finally sank in. Gradually, I began turning my attention back to music and singing.

During my junior year of high school, I began to feel like I was getting my life back. Little by little, my happiness and zeal for life returned. I started to expand my focus beyond my small community, and made the decision to attend high school in Amarillo, where I would stay with my mom's cousin Robin and her husband Shane.

There, I auditioned for an elite school choir and made the cut. I remember being so happy about that. Singing had filled me with joy as a little girl, and I realized that it also fed my soul as a teenager. I continued taking Spanish classes too, as I had been doing for a while, and even had a tutor come to the house a few times.

Robin told me years later that she and Shane would hide in the kitchen and eavesdrop. She laughed when telling me how funny I sounded speaking Spanish with a Texas twang. But hey, like everything else I did in life, I gave it my all—Lo di todo!

Part 2

Finding My Way

Going to Amarillo High School was the best decision I could have made. It helped me clear my head and gain new focus. I didn't know how I was going to make it happen, but I was looking toward a future of travel and music.

That was the same year Travis graduated from high school. His class asked me to sing at their graduation, and I happily agreed. I practiced and was ready to go, but on the afternoon of the graduation I was trembling with a bad case of nerves. Mom, being the "all natural hippie chick" she was, gave me some homeopathic calming drops to put under my tongue before I took the stage. She instructed me to take just a few drops, but I was so nervous that I drank the entire vial before going out to sing. That's me, always the overachiever.

The drops worked alright, because I was the picture of calm while singing my heart out for my brother's class. I was proud of my performance, and others seemed to enjoy it too. After my performance, I took my seat in the audience next to Mom.

She was beaming. "Wow! Those drops really worked!" She asked for the vial, and I placed it in her hand. She looked at the empty vial, then back at me. "Oh my God, Val! Did you take the whole vial!?"

Minutes later, I was so relaxed that I kept sliding down in my chair and couldn't keep my eyes open. Mom kept jabbing me with her elbow to wake me up.

The summer between my junior and senior year, I got a job working for an animal health company. While driving to work each day, I would dream of my magical future filled with music, art, and adventures. I was especially interested in traveling to Central and South America. I had an intense desire to live and experience everything life had to offer, and fully intended to do just that.

For my senior year, I returned to my hometown high school in Vega and graduated with the kids I'd grown up with. I enjoyed it, but missed Travis terribly. He was attending college twelve hours away. I spent a lot of time on the ranch dreaming of my future, but wasn't sure where to start. I began to look within myself for the answers.

High school was behind me, but I had no idea what college to attend. I couldn't seem to make up my mind, so Travis and Mom made it up for me. I would go to the same college Travis was attending: Stephen F. Austin University in Nacogdoches.

Moving away from home was good for me. New friends, new life, and a new town. I liked college and did very well. The best part was that Travis and I were together again.

I majored in International Business and Spanish and had more fun than should be allowed—it probably wasn't allowed, but remember I was Val Wonder and an overachiever.

I turned twenty-one in college, and threw myself a birthday party. I put up fliers all over campus and on the evening of the party it looked as though the entire campus had shown up. I had been doing some "legal drinking" earlier that day, and was fortunate that Travis was at the party. He could see that I needed to go back to my room, but was in no shape to get myself there. Turns out, his timing was perfect, because as soon as he had loaded me into his truck, the cops showed up.

After making our narrow escape, Travis got me back to my place but I was unable to climb the stairs up to my room. He threw me over his shoulder and carried me, whacking my head on the doorframe as we entered my room. My "room" was actually a large storage closet with a window that opened out onto the roof. He ended up staying all night, figuring that at some point I'd probably end up out there on the roof. I spent a lot of time on the roof looking up at the stars and planning my future. In fact, that's where I dreamed up Cheeky MaNeeky. I lost count of how many times my big brother rescued me, but that's just the kind of man he is and always has been. He was my eye in the middle of life's storm.

I had no idea what to do after college. I just kept dreaming about traveling, singing, creating art, and developing my character, Cheeky. And eating chocolate. Did I mention that I loved chocolate? By the time I graduated college, I had become somewhat of a chocolate connoisseur. I kept a box of the best I could find on hand, either in my car or my apartment. You know, for emergencies.

Travis and I graduated from college on the same day. We were in the coliseum, lined up to take the stage and receive our diplomas. I was right behind Travis, and we could see Mom waving at us from the audience. That's when it hit me—I didn't have my cap! I shot out of there like a bullet, drove across town and grabbed my cap, and made it back just in time to walk across the stage with Travis. He simply shook his head. I was smiling at the thrill of yet another challenge conquered. Another metaphor of how I lived my life.

Soon after graduating college, Mom got me a job with a medical device company in Dallas. When my family arrived to help me move, I had packed absolutely nothing. Oops. They weren't at all happy about that, and proceeded to stuff all my belongings into trash bags and load them onto Dad's horse trailer. I wasn't too concerned about domestic things at that point in my life. I took great care of Aspen, my black Lab, but my apartment not so much. So, the move was stressful and probably pretty hard on my parents.

My job at the medical device company was interesting, but I couldn't stop dreaming about traveling. I bought a shower curtain with a map of the world on it and would lie in the bath gazing at the map, dreaming of where I would travel to. Naturally, I got bored with the job pretty quickly. It wasn't a bad job, and the people were great, but it just wasn't what I wanted to do. And while I loved my apartment and my neighbors, my dreams were a fire in my soul that would not be quenched.

Some people used vision boards to visualize their dreams. I would transform my physical environment for the same reason. I was enthralled with the vibrant colors of South America, so I talked my cousin Hillary into helping me paint my apartment in a variety of crazy colors. She was attending grad school in the city and we got to hang out together often. We painted the entire apartment, and it looked amazing. I'm pretty sure that's why I didn't get my deposit back when I moved, but it was worth it.

This was a time in my life when I went through a period of rapid personal growth. I began studying yoga, spirituality, and ecology. My eyes opened to the fact that we were the keepers of Earth and our souls. I grew more passionate about the environment and realized that my apartment building wasn't doing its part to care for the Earth. I called Mom and asked if she thought I could start a recycling program for my building. She said, "Well Val, if anyone can do that it's you."

I guess she was right, because soon afterwards I talked my neighbors into helping me start that recycling program. I was all about implementing whatever I was learning, and didn't waste a lot of time mulling it over.

I made friends everywhere I went, on purpose. I hosted many dinner parties at my place and invited the most unique people I could find. One night, I made Paella from scratch for several random people from my apartment building. I shopped for the ingredients at a nearby Whole Foods and met a girl who worked there. I thought she was cool and invited her to dinner too. I believed one couldn't have too many diverse friends, and intentionally made as many as I could.

Living in a large city like Dallas helped me realize how much I loved being outside in nature. After all, I was a farm girl and living in a big city made me feel closed in. Plus, I felt like I was being smothered by a run-of-the-mill job. It just didn't fit into the person I was becoming or the life I wanted to build. I had to make a change. Living on my own, and away from the familiarity of my hometown, served as a catalyst that ignited a lot of my personal growth. I was becoming my own person, filled with passion for the dreams held in my heart, and was determined to make them happen.

A few months later, I quit my position at the medical device company, started picking up odd jobs, and began saving money for travel. In my spare time, I started a business plan for Cheeky MaNeeky, and continued to develop her character.

I left Dallas and moved to Vail, Colorado, to work at a ski resort. All the while, I kept saving my money, because I was determined to fulfill my dreams of traveling. Lindsey, a good friend I met in college, saw the fun life I was living and decided to move to Vail too. It was a special time for our friendship, and the perfect opportunity to expand our horizons together. We had so many fun adventures.

I invited Hillary and her fiancé to visit me in Vail. I told them they could stay with me and we'd go skiing at the four different resorts in the area. They drove all the way from Dallas to be with me. I probably should've mentioned that I was staying in employee housing with seven other people, but everything turned out okay. My roommates may have been a little annoyed with me, but I was happy to spend time with family.

Eventually, I decided to sell most everything I owned to fund my travel plans. I even sold the car Mom had bought for me. After all, I didn't need a car to travel the world. I posted the car for sale on the internet and accepted a cash offer from some dude I didn't know. I talked Hillary into going with me to meet him in a grocery store parking lot. For the record, Hillary thought it was a really bad idea. We drove in separate vehicles to the grocery store, and found him waiting with two other guys. He gave me the cash, and I quickly jumped into Hillary's car and locked the door. Needless to say, my family was not overjoyed when they heard about that sale.

I was happy though. There was finally enough money to travel. I got a teaching job in Buenos Aires, Argentina, and booked my flight. A good friend offered to dog-sit Aspen while I was away. Some might have said that I was being impulsive, but to me this was determination. I was determined to make the things I'd been dreaming about a reality, and I knew that wishing they would happen would never work. It was time for Val Wonder to take action.

Once again it was Hillary to the rescue, chauffeuring me to the airport. She couldn't believe that all I was taking with me was one bag and my giant snowboard. She made me pose for pictures, saying that she might need them to give to the U.S. Embassy when I went missing. That made me laugh.

I wasn't scared to travel alone. After all, Travis and I had gone to Hong Kong, Macau, and China by ourselves when I was fifteen. I figured Argentina would be a piece of cake in comparison. Some people probably thought Mom was crazy for letting us travel to Asia by ourselves, but that trip changed our lives. We both saw the world differently after that trip, and it fanned the flames of adventure in our hearts.

Now, I was feeling as though I had turned a page in my life. A whole new chapter was about to be written—from that point forward I would write my own story. After all, if you live your life trying to become who others think you should be, you'll end up miserable and unhappy. I wasn't going to live my life like that.

In Argentina, I stayed in a hostel with other expats. I found myself surrounded by different sights, smells, people, and experiences. Every minute was an adventure and I loved it. The job turned out to not be all it was cracked up to be, which made it hard financially, but I loved being there anyway.

One day, when some friends and I were in the downtown square in Buenos Aires, a man approached me and stole my purse at knifepoint. Along with my purse went my identification and money. I was crushed. It was a traumatic experience to say the least, and the local police were of no help. I went to the U.S. Embassy to see what they could do, which wasn't a lot either. They asked if I still had my passport, and I did. Thankfully, I had left it at the house where I was staying. Since I had my passport, I could still travel, which was a huge relief. Losing your passport in another country is a big hassle, so at least I didn't have to go through all of that.

A few weeks later, I made the decision to go back to the United States and regroup. It was summer in Argentina, which meant school was out and I didn't have the teaching job. My experiences in South America didn't deter me one bit. I loved my time there, except for being robbed of course, but wanted to go home and work on my next plan. I Skyped with my family, including Hillary, and let them know of my plan to return to the States. It was cheaper to fly home from Chile, rather than Argentina, so I boarded a rickety old bus and rode it all the way across the country and into Chile. If you've ever seen a movie where there was an American lost in another country, they're trying to get home, and find themselves riding an old bus filled with locals, their various belongings, and even some chickens— that was me. What an adventure!

Mom later told me how worried she had been about my return trip. She knew nothing of how I was getting to Chile, the flight numbers, or any other details. I never meant to cause anyone to worry, but I had a plan—there was always a plan.

I flew back to the United States and landed in Albuquerque, New Mexico. It turned out that I had a long layover, and extra time on my hands. There was also some money left from my trip to South America. Money and time —always a dangerous combination.

I'd never been happy with my thin lips, and with both time and money on my hands, I decided to do something about it. I looked up a local plastic surgeon and made an appointment to get lip injections. They talked me into doing lip implants instead. Naturally, my response was, "Why not?"

By the time I left the doctor's office, my lips were so swollen I could barely talk. I called Mom to check in and told her what I'd done. She wasn't overjoyed with the news.

I needed a few days for my lips to heal before Mom saw me, and decided to fly to Dallas to stay at Hillary's place. I took a cab from the airport to her apartment and knocked on the door. She opened the door and her expression went from surprise to shock.

"Hey Meeks!" (My nickname for her.) "I need a place to crash for a few days."

She was speechless, and for a couple of reasons. First was my unexpected arrival. She knew I was coming back to the States, but had no idea when, or that I was going to show up at her apartment. The second reason was the sight of my swollen lips. She freaked out, thinking my lips were swollen from the robbery incident in Argentina. I explained, and we had a good laugh about it. She let me stay, of course, but that was Hillary. She was always accepting of me, even when I was doing weird, unpredictable things, which was most of the time. I could always count on her, and hope she knows how much that meant to me.

A few days later I flew to Amarillo, where I stayed for a few weeks to recover from my lip implant fiasco. I also needed the time to decide what my next move would be. When I left Amarillo I headed to Taos, a small town in the high desert of northern New Mexico. Taos is surrounded by the Sangre de Cristo Mountains, and it's a magical place filled with lots of art and historic adobe buildings. I spent a few weeks there visiting a couple of relatives. Then I moved back to Breckenridge, Colorado. By that time it was 2009, and I was happy to be back in the Rocky Mountains. I had made several friends there and was glad to reconnect with them.

Some people probably thought I bounced around a lot, or viewed me as indecisive, but this way of living was intentional. I had to live and experience life firsthand, and that meant going to new places and meeting new people. My feeling was that too many people form a rigid world-view, having never ventured away from their familiar surroundings. I had to go out and see it all for myself. It never crossed my mind to live any other way. Life moves, every living thing has movement, and what does not move stagnates.

I took a bartending job at the Breckenridge Ski Resort, and it was a blast. It was like a party every night and I made so many friends. If you happen to visit the resort, check to see if they still have a drink on the menu called Valentini. I concocted it myself, and the manager liked it so much that she put it on the menu!

I loved my time in Breckenridge. I lived with a girl who worked with me at the resort, and Travis came to stay with us for about six months. He worked for UPS while he was there, and slept on our couch. We all went snowboarding as often as possible. Mom even visited us. It was such an amazing time. I was living a dream and having the time of my life.

Of course, I could only spend so much time in one place before I got the itch to move again. By 2010, I was feeling the urge, and moved to Denver, Colorado. I picked up a couple of odd jobs as a waitress and a personal assistant. My plans were the same, in that my goal was to work and save money for more traveling.

Funny story: While I was living in Denver, Dad came to visit and we decided to travel to Wyoming to see Travis. It was always good to reconnect with my brother after having been apart for a while. After we'd exchanged hugs and did some catching up, Travis informed us that he had to work the next day. He suggested that Dad and I go on a little fishing trip about an hour north, where the Teton Mountain Range began. There was a lake there that was created by a meteor a million or so years ago.

Dad and I made our way there the next day, me packing lunch and Dad packing the fishing gear. I was always eager when visiting new places and as we walked to the lake, I was pretty far ahead of Dad. We were walking a trail through dense willow thickets, with only a few clearings here and there. Dad had lost sight of me until he rounded a bend in the trail and came upon one of the clearings. He was shocked to see me running toward him in full retreat.

I ran up to him, eyes wide, and talking in a frantic but hushed manner. "There's a moose, Dad!"

At that moment, there were loud crashing noises behind me as the huge beast tried to escape. Using his enormous antlers, he cleared a path through the thicket to the lake, and swam to the other side. We stood there, staring at each other in disbelief. Suddenly, Dad's expression changed and I knew something was wrong.

Behind me, and way too close, stood a moose cow and her calf. Mama moose was staring us down, not at all happy that we were so close to her baby. Dad whispered to carefully turn to the side and slowly walk away. We did so, with the mother's eyes on us the entire time. I was terrified, but began formulating escape plans in case she charged us. I suggested we jump in the lake and swim out to the overflow cage in the middle of the lake. Dad found that kind of funny, and asked if that was the best plan I could come up with. I gave him one of my trademarked, "You got anything better?" looks and punched him in the arm. We managed to escape unharmed, and spent the rest of the day fishing.

We returned to Travis' house later that day, and I couldn't wait to tell him the story. He thoroughly enjoyed my recount, and my added embellishments made for some good entertainment. I share that story because it perfectly illustrates something I experienced many times: it's often the unexpected adventures in life that you treasure the most. As a side note, I'd like to point out that even during an emergency situation I was trying to formulate a plan.

I loved living in Denver, but it wasn't long before I had the urge to be on the move again. My next destination was California, where I went to work during the marijuana harvest season. It was known as "going to weed camp," and it really was a camp where we lived in tents. I made some great money working there, and made some amazing friends who would remain in my circle for the rest of my life. In fact, that's where I met Joshua Finley, who would become my art partner and beloved friend. I remember calling Mom and telling her about the cool guy I met while "camping."

When weed camp was over I headed back to Taos, and to my aunt and uncle's house for a few days. I'd been camping and harvesting for a few weeks, so the first thing they did was "decontaminate" me by washing all of my belongings so I wouldn't wreak of weed. They got such a kick out of my condition when I arrived. After my "Taos

Cleanse," I headed back to Denver. Travis joined me there for a while.

Once again, I picked up odd jobs and spent time getting to know Josh and his artistic mind. We talked endlessly about Cheeky, the character I had invented and wanted to write about. He had some great ideas and began to experiment with drawing Cheeky and her friends.

Before the dust could settle though, I was already thinking of moving to New York City. That had been a dream of mine for a long time, and I was determined to make it happen. I sublet my Denver apartment to Joey and Amanda. That was the beginning of a wonderful friendship. Amanda and I spent countless hours talking about Cheeky and between the two of us, we came up with dozens of ideas. After my diagnosis, Amanda was one of the few people I wanted to spend time with.

2010 came and went and by 2011, I was living in New York City. One of my college roommates, Jenna, lived there and I was excited about reconnecting with her. I wasn't in the city long before I became friends with a highly accomplished musician named Dru. We ended up sharing an apartment together with one other person. Dru was a Buddhist and I would often sit with him during his spiritual meditations. We would talk for hours about spirituality, God, and our purpose in life.

Living in New York was exciting, and I explored the city as much as possible. I picked up some waitressing jobs and even worked at Hell's Kitchen for a while. A few months after my move, Josh joined me there. He loved it. We continued to develop his art business and talk about Cheeky's future.

One day, we were on the subway and Josh was sketching different pictures of Cheeky in his notebook. We were working to develop just the right image for her. When we got off the subway, Josh paused near one of the underground pillars and continued sketching Cheeky on the pillar. When he was finished, we both looked at the drawing and said, "That's it! That's Cheeky!" The character you now see in all of the *Cheeky MaNeeky* books was born that day in a New York City subway station.

At one point, Robin and Shane came for a visit. It was a hot summer. One afternoon, after spending the day doing touristy things, we decided to head back to their hotel and cool off in the pool before going out for dinner. All I had brought with me was my purse, but everything I needed was crammed in there, including my swimsuit. After the swim I took a shower. Everyone was shocked when I donned a dress and different shoes. I had even put on make-up and fixed my hair.

Robin and Shane just stared, mouths open, and asked, "Where were you hiding this wardrobe?"

I reminded them that as a frequent traveler, I'd learned how to get the most out of a purse. I'd learned to be adaptable. The more adaptable you can be, the easier you can adjust to new situations and circumstances. It makes life a little easier, and a lot less stressful.

By late 2011, I was beginning to feel closed in by the city. I was a farm girl, accustomed to wide open spaces, and decided to go back to Denver. Josh loved living in New York City, and had been immersed in his art and painting murals. Reluctantly, he agreed to go with me. We moved into an apartment in Wash Park, a cool neighborhood in Denver. Josh worked on his art, and I helped him by working on the business end of things, as well as working odd jobs.

Cheeky MaNeeky

We carried on that way for several months, but life never became a rut for me because I would change things up before that could happen. When harvest time rolled around again in California, we decided to go back to "weed camp." It was a great way to make some serious money, and since we both grew up on a farm we knew how to work hard.

I sublet my Denver apartment to a friend, Andrea, and took off for Cali. Somehow, in the midst of all the preparations to leave, I forgot to tell Travis I was going. He came to Denver to visit, only to find me gone and someone else staying in my apartment. On the bright side, he got to meet my friend Andrea. She took it all in stride. When Travis showed up at the apartment she said, "Well, if you're Val's brother you're welcome here!" Oops.

In 2013, I got serious about developing Josh's art business, and wrote a business plan and built a website. I also continued to work on the business plan for Cheeky MaNeeky. I would tell Josh the stories I came up with, and he would illustrate them. I also created a few songs that Cheeky would sing. Josh and I worked well together, and things were going well for our creative endeavors. Creativity was more than an outlet for me, and certainly more than a hobby. Creating art and writing were as necessary for me as breathing. Without it, life began to wither and stagnate.

The following year, we traveled to my hometown of Vega, to paint a few murals. Located in the Texas Panhandle, Vega is a small town of less than a thousand people, situated along Route 66. We stayed with Mom for the entire summer, which was great. It was during this time that Josh began teaching me the techniques for painting murals. I learned so much from him, and because I was an artist too, I was a quick study.

Several people would stop by and watch us work. We even let my mom paint a bush on one of the murals, though Josh did touch it up a bit afterwards. We painted several murals, and if you ever pass through Vega, be sure to stop by the Milburn-Price Culture Museum. The museum itself is cool, with so many interesting things to see, and they also have a map that shows where all of the murals are located around town.

Though things were going well, as far as our art was concerned, Josh and I decided to go our separate ways in the fall of 2014. It was a hard decision, and I think we both felt a little lost at that point. I believe we both understood that in order for each of us to move forward in our lives, it meant we'd have to walk different paths. Nevertheless, it was an agonizing time.

I needed some time away from everything, and had to figure out what to do next. I also needed time to think and process my feelings. Jenna, my former college roommate, was planning to get married in September. The wedding was going to be in the outskirts of London, and I was asked to be one of the bridesmaids. The timing couldn't have been better, and soon I was on a plane to the UK. The wedding was beautiful, and guess who caught the bouquet! Little did I know that my world was about to turn upside down, in a good way!

There's a tradition in Britain, where the woman who catches the bride's bouquet shares a dance with the man who catches the garter. That dance happened, and the fireworks soon followed. His name was Nathan, and our connection was instantaneous. I spent the next two weeks in the UK and Spain, and it was glorious. Nathan joined me in Spain where we shared a few romantic and magical days together.

When I returned to Denver from that amazing trip, I was on cloud nine. I needed those two weeks to clear my head and regroup, but it wasn't easy leaving Nathan.

I told Mom all about the man from Wales I met at Jenna's wedding. I couldn't wait to see him again. But even with all of that going on, I didn't get sidetracked from developing my Cheeky MaNeeky character, creating art, and writing songs. There was a river of creativity flowing within me and nothing could slow it down or dam it up— not even me.

My brother and his soon-to-be bride, Becky, called one day to let me know about an opportunity in their town of Rock Springs, Wyoming. The city was looking for artists to paint a huge mural in the downtown area. I was intrigued, but wasn't sure about painting something that large. I scrolled through Facebook, while pondering whether or not to attempt the mural, and came across a post from Josh's new mural partner. The post stated that while they were painting a mural, someone drove by and fired a gun at them. The bullet narrowly missed Josh and lodged itself in the brick wall of the building. I was stunned, and immediately grabbed my phone and called Josh.

We ended up having a long-overdue conversation. It was good to reconnect with him, and that call began a resurgence of our creative force.

I decided to place my bid for the mural gig in Rock Springs, after a lot of help and instruction from Josh about how to do the proposal. I won the bid and was off for Wyoming to paint a mural during the winter. It was to be the first-ever mural in downtown Rock Springs.

Valerie working on the mural in
Rock Springs, Wyoming.

Valerie & Travis

What had I gotten myself into? I seemed to have a way of putting myself into uncomfortable situations, but then again, that's the only way you can grow as a person. You only get out of life what you're willing to pour into it. So, when life presented me with an opportunity, my response was almost always a resounding yes. I would figure out the rest later.

For the next two months, I stayed with Travis and Becky while working on the mural. There were days when I would procrastinate, and Travis would motivate me by saying, "You better get it done, the really cold weather is coming."

It was a huge project and I was working alone. I made at least forty-seven trips to the home improvement store to get paint. There was no way I would finish the mural before the temperature plummeted. When it gets that cold, paint doesn't dry, which is a serious problem. Once again, big brother came to my rescue. He figured out a way to hang heavy plastic over my working area and the scaffolding. Inside the plastic cocoon he placed heaters and lights. Without his help and hard work, I would've never finished that job. How many times had that scenario played out in my life? I would get in over my head, or get caught way out on a limb somewhere, and Travis would swoop in and rescue me. How fortunate I was to have such an amazing human for a brother, and a best friend for life.

It took a while, and there were times when it seemed that my hands would freeze and fall off, but I finished the mural. It turned out great and I was so proud of it. You'll never know your true potential until you push yourself, and painting that massive mural alone showed me what I was capable of as an artist. I even made the front page of the *Rocket Miner!*

With the mural complete, I headed back to Denver. Right after I arrived, I received an offer to paint another mural in Vega, so back to Texas I went. I painted the mural during the Christmas holidays of 2014, but it was so much warmer there than it had been in Wyoming. Mom would drop by sometimes to help me, and I would talk to her nonstop about Nathan.

Words couldn't describe how deeply I was in love with him. We talked on the phone every day, and took turns flying back and forth to see each other.

When 2015 arrived, it brought with it a lot of changes. Mom moved into a new house she had built and started a new life, alone. I offered to paint some original art for her house that was specific to her personality. She agreed, and I began working on five large paintings.

I know most daughters would say that they love their mother, but the deep bond I shared with my mom was indescribable. She was my best friend, confidant, and source of unconditional love. And when things got tough, she was my rock. I wanted to give back to her what she had always given me, at least in some measure. I would often tell her that when she got old, I would take care of her. She'd smile and call me sweet, but I really meant it. Travis and I had long ago decided that when Mom retired, she would move close to me so I could look after her. We even talked her into coming to Denver once to check out some areas where she might like to live. I had her retirement life all planned out!

Mom let me know that I brought up the subject of her retirement frequently. Perhaps the reason it was on my mind so much was because I was manifesting a man for her. I didn't want her to be lonely. I used to call her and give her progress updates on the paintings. During one of those calls, I spilled the beans about my plan to manifest the perfect person for her.

She responded with, "Oh Val, I don't need a man. I'm fine."

I was undeterred. I was still trying to find a way for Nathan and I to live together on the same continent, and that made me think of Mom even more. No matter what happened, I wanted to be sure she was okay and not alone.

By the time July came around, I had finished Mom's paintings. We decided to meet at a pizza place in Trinidad, Colorado, and spend the day together. She asked if I would mind if she brought Jimmy with her, a man whom she had been seeing. He had a pickup that would easily transport the five large paintings, and he wanted to meet me. Of course, I was fine with it. In fact, I told Mom that I already knew all about him. I had never seen a picture of him, but knew what he looked like because he was the man I had manifested for her.

Mom was skeptical, but when we met in Trinidad, I walked right up to Jimmy. I didn't need an introduction because I knew exactly who he was. We connected instantly, and talked for a long time. At one point, I think Mom wandered outside as Jimmy and I kept talking. The three of us had a great afternoon together. Oh, and Mom loved the paintings too.

I left Trinidad with a smile on my face. I was happy and grateful that Mom had found someone special, and it felt good knowing she would be cared for if I ended up moving far away. As I drove back to Denver, I called to let Mom know how happy I was to have met Jimmy, and that she loved my paintings. She paid me, but seeing her joy is what made it worthwhile.

Back in Denver, I continued to work on commissioned art projects. I also helped out a friend by working in her restaurant, all while continuing to develop Cheeky Ma-Neeky. I was determined to see that vision through and impact the lives of children with positive lessons via Cheeky's exploits.

Nathan was always on my mind. We spoke regularly, trying to weave together a solid plan to be together. I decided to sell my condo and prepare to move to the UK. The situation was complicated because I wasn't a citizen of Great Britain and Nathan wasn't a citizen of the United States. No matter which one of us moved, work visas were going to be a pain to deal with.

There was never a time in my life when Mom wasn't there for me, and I'd call her often to talk about everything. There was a lot going on during that time, and I found myself getting short with her, sometimes even angry. A few times I got so upset that I'd yell and hang up, only to call her back and apologize. That wasn't like me, and I thought that perhaps the stress of everything was getting to me.

I felt overwhelmed and exhausted, and was unable to concentrate. Mom was worried, and told me so. Like me, she thought I was stressed out over doing too many things all at once. She thought I should put the Cheeky MaNeeky project on hold for a month so I could concentrate on selling my condo and making plans with Nathan. The problem was that I would get something in my head and couldn't stop thinking about it. It was driving me crazy.

As the next couple of months unfolded, I burned the candle at both ends. I was exhausted all the time, but couldn't make myself stop. During the last two weeks of October, I called Mom often and we got into arguments over everything. That wasn't normal for us at all, and I asked her if I was going crazy. She didn't think I was, but did say I could have a hormone imbalance or something.

Whatever the case, I wasn't acting like myself and she asked if I could come to see her soon. "Sometimes a girl just needs to see her mom," she said.

I agreed.

It was a Friday evening near the end of October when we agreed that I would leave for Texas and arrive at her house on Monday afternoon. The plan was for me to get there around four o'clock, about the time she got off work. Mom wanted to get me in to see a doctor. I didn't know if there was an issue or not, but I was relieved to be going home.

Of course, something must've been wrong. I was sleeping too much, arguing with Mom, and getting bad headaches—I never got headaches. Something was off and I couldn't put my finger on it, but I knew the decision to go home was the right one. I needed help, and Mom would know what to do.

I don't really know how things unfolded over the next couple of days. My memory was fuzzy and there was a lot of confusion. I simply remember throwing some things in a suitcase, grabbing Aspen, and leaving.

Somehow, I made it to Mom's house. It was Monday and Mom was expecting me, but not for another twelve hours. She was getting ready for work when Aspen and I walked in at four-thirty in the morning. Mom was visibly shaken. I had lost a lot of weight, and wasn't acting like myself. Aspen was acting strangely too, and seemed almost relieved to be there. It was November and cold, yet I arrived wearing a tank top, cutoff jeans, and flip-flops.

Aspen & Valerie

Naturally, Mom was worried. She asked me several questions, and all I could muster was, "Mom, I'm so tired. I just need to sleep."

Aspen and I headed to bed, and Mom said she'd get my luggage from my car. She picked up my purse to move it and found it empty, except for my driver's license and a Target credit card. Her concern only deepened when she went to my car and found it freezing inside. I had driven for six hours, dressed in summer clothes, without heat. She retrieved my suitcase, and found that it contained a hodgepodge of dirty clothes, mismatched outfits, and no personal products at all. I had also not brought any dog food for Aspen, who only ate organic food. I took great care of Aspen, and never went anywhere without her food and vitamins. It was all very surreal, like I was living in a dream—one that I wanted to awaken from, but couldn't.

Mom went on to work and I slept for most of the day. By the time she got home later that afternoon, I was feeling a little better. I remember going to my car and retrieving an armload of mail. I handed it all to Mom because I didn't know what to do with it. She was shocked to see it was all unopened, and that I hadn't paid bills for the last two months. It was like I couldn't reason out the simplest things, yet instinctively knew to lean on Mom. I wish every person had someone like my mom in their life. She was always there for me, no matter the circumstances, and whenever life got hard, I knew she would be my rock.

The following day I saw a few relatives, including my dad, Hillary, and her newborn son. I began to gather some art supplies, because art kept me grounded and in tune with who I was. I had a huge canvas to paint as a commissioned piece and wanted to start painting as soon as possible. The rest of the day was pretty much uneventful, and it seemed things might be settling down. All of that changed the next day.

It was a typical Wednesday morning. Mom was up at four o'clock to get ready for work, and I got up to do some painting for a client. Jimmy had set up a makeshift art studio for me in Mom's garage, complete with lights and heaters. He also took care of my car, which quite frankly, I'm not sure how it survived the drive to Texas. I had been neglecting almost everything.

I felt pretty good and was optimistic about the day. Mom was only working until noon because she had scheduled a doctor's appointment for me. I was fine with that because I wanted to figure out why I had been feeling so strange for the past several weeks.

Mom left for work and I started painting. I remember going into the closet to grab something and then suddenly it was an hour later and I was waking up on the floor. What happened? I was dazed and felt dried drool on my chin. I couldn't see out of my right eye. Where had the last hour gone? I burst into tears. Had I fallen and hit my head? I was terrified. Still in tears, I called Mom at work. She listened as I tried to explain what was going on.

"Stay right where you are and I will be there as soon as I can," she told me.

It seemed like forever, but Mom finally came home. She took one look at my confused expression and the dried drool on my face, and knew I'd had a seizure. She had seen post-seizure behavior many times during her career as a nurse, and she knew the signs. What Mom didn't know was why. She thought maybe I had fallen and hit my head. Fearing a severe concussion or brain bleed, she rushed me to the emergency room.

Part 3

Embracing Uncertainty

"Honey, I have bad news. There's a tumor in your brain and it's big."

Mom's words hung heavy in the air and time stood still. My initial response was stunned silence. With everything I'd been experiencing, I knew something wasn't right, but when Mom spoke those words to me, I couldn't believe it. There was so much going on in my life—things I wanted to do, places to see. I was in love.

Of course, that must be how it is for everyone. Is anyone ever ready for their life to end? For most people, the answer is no, and that's a good thing. You *should* be about the business of living, right up to your last breath. You should be more concerned with filling your days with living and less concerned with how long you live. Like the old adage says, "It's not the years in your life that count, but the life in your years."

I wasn't thinking any of that in the moments following my diagnosis. I was scared and devastated. I was only thirty years old and had just been told that I'd be lucky if I made it to thirty-one.

After Mom had delivered the shocking news, several doctors and nurses poured into the room. Most of them had worked with her at some point, and wanted to show their support. But it was overwhelming. All of it. While they were there, and Mom knew I wouldn't be alone, she left the room to make some phone calls. She called Jimmy and let him know what was going on. He arrived at the hospital within thirty minutes. After calling Jimmy, she came to check on me, and I asked her to call Nathan.

Nathan was still in the UK, so Mom used WhatsApp on her phone to make the call. Up until that time, she had never spoke with Nathan. What a way to meet, right? She stepped out of the room to make the call. He was at work when she called, but he answered. After introducing herself and apologizing for the circumstances, she filled him in on my trip to the ER, as well as the MRI results. Nathan was a physical therapist so he understood what was going on. He asked to speak with me. I mostly cried as we talked, but was happy to hear his voice. It was so soothing and calming to me. Nathan said he would get a flight to the States as soon as possible.

I gave the phone back to Mom and she called my dad and Travis. Travis' fiancé, Becky, answered their phone. She told Mom that Travis was up in the mountains hunting and didn't have cell phone reception. Later that evening, after reaching an area with good reception, he received Mom and Becky's messages. He called Mom and got the details, then literally left the mountains right that moment. He drove straight home and was on a plane to Texas within two days. To arrange that in two days is almost impossible, but then again, it's Travis we're talking about. He was always there when I needed him.

In the afternoon, they moved me to a private room. Dad arrived later that evening, and so did many others. They came from Dallas, Denver, Brownfield, Vega, Lubbock, and several other places. The room was packed with friends.

Seeing them all lifted my spirits. I was able to laugh and joke with them, and felt more like myself. Never underestimate the power that comes from being surrounded by people who love you.

One of the doctors Mom had worked with closely, asked to speak with her. They left the room and walked down the hallway to a room where they could talk in private. This man wasn't my doctor. He was a good friend of ours, and wanted to kindly break the bad news to Mom. I appreciated the respect and compassion he had for my family.

"D'Ann, this is bad. Real bad. The tumor is fast-moving and it's terminal. We don't have good treatments for this."

They sat there together and cried for several minutes. He let her know that my neurosurgeon would be in to speak with her soon. They gathered themselves, and as they were leaving, they ran into him in the hallway.

The surgeon took Mom aside and gave her the grim details. Besides this being the most aggressive type of cancer, it was also wrapped around my optic nerve. He recommended surgery to confirm the diagnosis and remove as much of the tumor as possible, but even that would only buy me so much time. Mom asked him about additional treatment options. The only things available were chemo and radiation. The surgeon also advised that I be put on anti-seizure medication, and steroids for the swelling in my brain.

Mom told the surgeon that they needed to discuss everything with me, knowing that I would likely not want to take the chemo and radiation route. They came to my room and asked everyone to step out for a few minutes. The surgeon laid it all out for me, and I listened silently. What *could* I say? I just wanted out of the hospital and told him so. He said that if I did okay that night, I could go home the next morning.

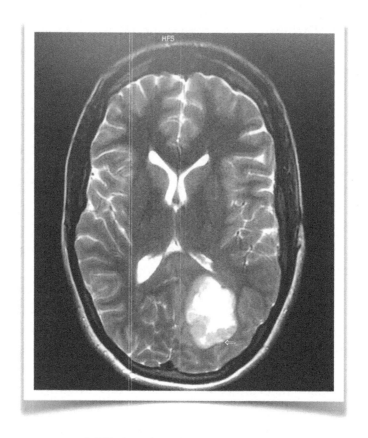

MRI showing the brain tumor.

The surgeon left and my friends and family returned. At that point, I was feeling agitated and completely overwhelmed. When the nurse brought the medication, I refused to take it. When they brought food, I refused to eat it. There's nothing healthy about hospital food anyway, which is kind of ironic when you think about it. Mom tried to talk me into taking the medication, but I wouldn't do it. It felt like my whole world was spinning out of control and I just wanted it to stop. One of Mom's friends, Patti, tried to talk me into taking the medication, but I had already made up my mind. I would seek alternative treatments outside of mainstream medicine.

Later that night, everyone left except for Mom. I could see how everything that was happening was taking a heavy toll on her. She burst into tears, telling me how sorry she was about what I was going through it. What impacts you will affect those who care about you, and in that moment the impact on my mother was tremendous.

Mom crawled into bed beside me, and we cried for a long time. I couldn't shake the feeling that this was all some kind of mistake. When the flood of emotions began to subside, I started to see pieces of a larger picture. Once the news of my condition spread, my family and friends would be worried and scared. It pained me to know how much they'd be hurting, and that understanding helped me see that what was happening wasn't just about me.

It's only natural to think of yourself when something like this happens in your life. But you don't walk through life as an island. There are people you know and love, not to mention your family, and all of them will feel deeply what's happening to you. It's not easy—not even close— but if you can grasp this truth you will find that there is even meaning in death.

I didn't intend to give up though. I would fight for my life with every ounce of strength I possessed, and in a way that would show others that beauty can still be present in every minute of their lives, no matter what storm they might have to endure.

Seeing Mom cry was heartbreaking, and I began to cry too. She laid in bed with me and held me as we wept. The bond we shared was strong, but in that moment, it grew even stronger.

I choked back my tears and said, "Mom, you know my umbilical cord is attached to you again, right?"

She nodded. "And that's where you need to be."

You know, there's something special about a mother's connection to her children. It's a connection that isn't severed when the umbilical cord is cut, and it lasts a lifetime. My mother told me that if it were possible, she would trade places with me in a heartbeat. I had no doubt that she would.

We talked about the surgery, and I told her that I would *not* take any chemo or radiation treatments. Period. I had an appointment with my doctor a few days later, and she said we'd talk everything over with him at that time.

In those precious moments, while mother and daughter clung to each other in deep sadness, I began to get some clarity on a bigger picture. In the depths of the despair and anguish that gripped my heart, I began to wonder if it were possible for some good to come out of the situation.

I knew my ordeal would bring pain to many people, especially those close to me. I couldn't stop that from happening, but maybe I could inspire others in some way. I was only thirty years old, and knew people twice my age who had never really lived. They had spent the majority of their lives being afraid to take a chance, pursue a dream, or to love freely. If I could face what was happening to me, and still live from a place of love, maybe I could inspire someone to fully embrace the beautiful gift of being alive. Maybe I could inspire them to not fear death. It wasn't going to be easy. I had my own fears to conquer, but I had to try. I was devastated and scared, but determined to be like a rock cast into a pond, from which ripples would travel outward to the very edges. The rock may sink to the bottom, but the ripples go on.

We laid together in that hospital bed, hands clasped together, facing an uncertain future. But then, isn't the future always uncertain?

"Mom, I don't know why this is happening to me, but you know our job in all of this is to be an inspiration to others."

I spoke those words, but in some ways, it felt a little like I was on the outside looking in. It was like I was an observer of it all instead of a participant. Ultimately, I was both.

The next morning, I left the hospital and went to Mom's house. Lots of people came over to visit. Some called or messaged. Others emailed, wanting to know how I was doing and if they could help. It was a wonderful outpouring of support, and also a little overwhelming.

Mom and I had to come up with a plan and we didn't have much time to do it. The tumor was growing aggressively and we began researching options right away. Mom was a woman on a mission and kicked everything into high gear. She employed the help of several nurse friends. They all worked tirelessly to help me find the best path forward. I was grateful to all of them, especially Mom, because I was still in a state of shock and having a difficult time believing what was happening.

Nathan & Valerie

Nathan arrived the following weekend. Mom and Jimmy took me to the airport to pick him up. Instead of going back to Mom's, Nathan and I booked a room in a beautiful hotel. We needed time together and I needed time away from all the chaos. I was happy to be with him again. God, I loved him so much and having him with me was an incredible comfort. We talked about my upcoming surgery and alternative treatments, but mostly we just spent time together. It seemed as if we'd never had enough of that, and now were faced with the looming possibility that our future together would be cut short. Our time together offered much-needed peace and respite from the storm swirling around us.

The next day, we left the hotel and basically moved into Mom's house. I only had the personal items I brought with me from Denver, which was next to nothing. Several of my friends from Denver came streaming into Texas to see me, bringing things from my condo back in Colorado. Hillary came over, and together with her Mom, got to work organizing my room and closet space. It was mind-blowing how many people were pitching in to help. It's been said that the love you put out into the world comes back to you. I lived that truth during those days.

The next few days were a blur. There were friends and relatives visiting, calling, and pitching in to help. My first appointment with the surgeon was on a Friday, a few days after Nathan arrived. I went to the appointment with an entourage of friends and family: Nathan, Mom and Jimmy, Dad and his wife, Marianne. You know, facing something that is life-threatening is one of the most difficult things anyone can do, but if you ever have to go through, it I hope you're surrounded by people who love you like I was loved. I often said that love is the only thing that really matters, and the truth of that statement was revealed to me on a deeper level after my diagnosis. It's easy to be distracted by things like your career, money, paying bills, or a million other things, but when all of that is stripped anyway and it's just you standing alone staring into the abyss of eternity, it all becomes vividly clear. Without love, everything else loses its meaning.

The surgeon showed us the MRI results. This was the first time I had seen the tumor. It was huge, the size of an egg, and was located in the left occipital lobe, toward the back of my skull. It's one thing to talk about having a brain tumor, but actually seeing it is quite another. I listened to what the doctor had to say and made the decision to have surgery and remove as much of the tumor as possible. The surgeon informed me that the tumor was wrapped around my occipital nerve and that I'd lose most, if not all, of my vision.

It seemed like the bad news kept on coming. I was an artist and much of my creativity was expressed through visual media. Losing my sight would be a tremendous blow. Still, I would get through it. I wanted the tumor to be gone, and would deal with whatever consequences came afterwards.

The surgery was scheduled for November 10. Ironically, that was the date of my grandad's birthday and his death. It was a date that held significance for my family, and I found it interesting that my surgery would fall on the same day. The night before my surgery, several of my old friends showed up. It was almost like a party, except for the somber circumstances. I loved my friends and having them stand by me during the most difficult time of my life meant more than they would ever know, but everything was overwhelming at that time. There was so much going on, and things were happening so fast. I just wanted to disappear.

In preparation for my surgery, my friend Vanessa cut off my long hair. My eyes filled with tears as the scissors did their work. With each clump of hair that drifted to the floor, I felt as though I was losing a piece of myself. I was losing everything. I couldn't drive, everything I owned was in Denver, privacy was a thing of the past, and now my long, beautiful hair was taken from me. In a week's time, my way of life was completely wiped out. The next morning, I would likely lose my vision. What else did I have left to give?

We got up early the next morning and went to the hospital. The whole gang went with me and filled the waiting room. When the nurse came out to get me, the tension in the room was so heavy it was palpable. Mom was about to burst into tears, and everyone else was visibly nervous and worried. Of course, we all hoped for the best possible outcome—that after the surgery, the surgeon would announce that the tumor hadn't been a grade 4 glioblastoma after all, but simply a benign growth. Despite our best wishes, our worst fears were confirmed.

During my surgery the waiting room was packed with friends and family. One of my friends had T-shirts printed with Team Valerie and Val Wonder, and many were wearing them. After they waited for what seemed like an eternity, the surgeon entered the room. He walked directly over to Mom. From his somber expression, she knew the worst-case scenario was about to be confirmed.

He addressed both Mom and Dad. "The surgery went well. About seventy-five percent of the tumor was removed, but it's very likely that the surgery has affected her occipital nerve. The next twelve to twenty-four hours

75

will reveal if she has retained her vision. I'm sorry to say that the diagnosis is confirmed. The tumor is a grade 4 glioblastoma."

Mom couldn't hold her tears any longer, and felt as though she'd pass out. Dad cried too. Nathan had disappeared from the waiting room. I can't imagine what he went through. He was in a country where he knew almost no one, had flown in just days before, and was probably still jet-lagged from the trip. Not to mention, the stress over what was happening to me. He must've felt so alone. Mom went looking for him and found him in a different waiting room. He was on the phone updating his family on the latest news. Mom said he was pretty quiet after the call and just wanted to see me.

I was moved to the ICU, where my family was able to see me for a few minutes. When I finally awoke, I had no vision whatsoever for twelve hours. I was told to expect that, because the surgery stunned my optic nerve, but the question was how much of my vision would return. It was scary and surreal. Nathan never left my side. He sat next to the bed and held my hand. Keeping me calm for the rest of the day and all through the night.

The next day I regained some of my sight, but there were spots of blackness and everything was blurry. I could only see people if I turned my head sideways. I had a killer headache, but otherwise felt okay. I was transferred to a regular room, and within a few days I was discharged.

You know how after someone has surgery, they go back home and spend their time recovering? The worst is usually over and all that's left is to heal and get on with life. Well, that's not how it was for me. After I returned to Mom's, we spent the next two weeks coming up with a treatment plan. I was firm in my decision to not have chemo and radiation.

The odds of its success were extremely low. Besides, the treatments would've more than likely been in Houston and I didn't want to waste the time I had left in treatments, being sick and away from my family.

Glioblastoma tumors are very aggressive, and even with chemo and radiation, most of the doctors agreed that treatment would give me just a couple of more months. The surgeon urged us to see an oncologist anyway. I resisted but Mom insisted. On the day of the appointment, Mom, Dad, and Marianne went with me. I asked the oncologist several questions, but he had no good answers. Later, Dad asked me to see a different oncologist. I refused, but once again, Mom insisted. So, off I went to another oncologist. That doctor didn't have any good answers either. In fact, I got so upset, that I walked out of the room. Mom followed me out into the lobby, but I was done.

I looked at Mom and said, "No more. I won't see another oncologist!"

Looking back, I know Mom was making sure that we explored every available option, but my mind was made up. Most mothers would've probably been upset to hear their daughter, who has a cancerous tumor, declare that she won't talk to another doctor. But my mom wasn't most mothers. Her response after my emphatic declaration?

"Okay. It's your body and your decision. I will support whatever you want."

Can you begin to grasp the strength she must've possessed in order to utter those words? She set aside any feelings she may have had about what I should do, and gave me full reign over my own life. Despite whatever thoughts Mom may have had, she allowed me to decide for myself without pressure or stress. I wish I could describe how much that meant to me. So often, when a loved one is facing a life-threatening illness, friends and family over-whelm them with advice and opinions. Their intentions are good, but I promise you, it doesn't help. Allow the ones you care about to retain their dignity. Be there if and when they need you, but give them all the space they need to deal with their situation.

I decided to take the holistic path, and Mom's help was invaluable. Mom had experienced her own healing journey a few years before when she battled an autoimmune disease. After much time consulting with doctors and several failed treatments, she created her own holistic treatment plan. She drew upon all of her experience to help me develop one of my own, and found three holistic medical doctors to help us formulate a course of action. I was actually feeling really good at this point, but my vision was terrible and my memory wasn't that great either.

I returned to the surgeon to have the eighteen stitches removed from my scalp on November 25. It happened to be the same day much of my family gathered at my Mom's house for Thanksgiving. My cousins Hillary and Joel were there, and I was happy to be with them. I remember that Travis, Joel, Hillary, and I posed for a picture that day. The pain we were all feeling was evident in the photo. It would be the last photo of the four of us together.

As the days passed, Mom coordinated all of the herbs, alternative medications, supplements, and food for my treatment plan. It was *my* plan and I was good with it. I went for multiple detox treatments, massages, biofeedback, and much more. Mom talked to all the practitioners, dealt with the insurance companies, and kept me on schedule. In the midst of all of that, she was still working at the hospital and trying to sell my condo in Denver.

Nathan helped Mom a lot. He was very supportive of my choices, and also reached out to medical professionals in the UK to explore any treatment options they might have to offer. That meant everything to me.

Travis was working hard on straightening out my finances. Before coming back to Texas to stay with Mom, I hadn't been dealing with my mail or bills for a couple of months. Everything was a mess.

I guess I'd let everything go because I couldn't focus and was so easily overwhelmed due to the tumor. Travis finally got it all in order and helped me keep it that way. He was living in Wyoming and flew to Texas to be with me many times during the months following my surgery. We were both so sad about everything that was happening. I loved him deeply, and he was my best friend. We still managed to find ways to laugh and be silly, just like when we were kids. It made me feel normal, if only for a while.

Of course (cue eye roll) none of the treatments I was on were paid for by insurance. Insurance companies only like to pay for toxic pharmaceuticals, invasive surgery, and harmful radiation. They reject anything organic, holistic, or otherwise. They wouldn't even cover my supplements or vitamins. And that's supposed to be health care? Needless to say, my treatments were expensive and paying for everything was a real concern. Some of Mom's friends wanted to do a fundraiser for me, and my friend Lindsey set up a GoFundMe page to help raise money.

I was deeply grateful for everyone who was helping me, but those days were overwhelmingly busy. I needed time to be alone and process what was happening. My journal became my sacred space, where I could pour out my thoughts and feelings. It helped a lot, but my rock in the middle of the storm was Nathan. His presence brought me calm and peace, two things I desperately needed at that time. I could no longer drive so Nathan drove us everywhere we had to go, and sometimes we just drove around. A few weeks after my surgery, he decided to fly back to the UK, move out of his apartment, and take a leave of absence from his job. It saddened me to see him go, but he assured me he would return as soon as possible.

The day he left, I felt so alone. I told Mom, "Either he will come back or he won't. I wouldn't blame him if he didn't return. This is very hard and stressful. He could fly back to the UK and we might never hear from him again."

I don't think I really believed he wouldn't return, but I was lost without him by my side. I just wanted everything to stop. I wanted to do my art. I wanted to be healthy and most of all, I wanted to have my life with Nathan. I wanted to press pause and reset my life, but that's not how it works. Life goes on, regardless of circumstances. Even in death, life still goes on.

The doctor had told us that without any treatment the tumor would grow rapidly. He said that I should expect a fifty percent growth by the time I had my next MRI in about six weeks. But, the best they could offer me after three months of toxic chemotherapy was the slim chance that I might live a month or so longer. Why would I put myself and my family through all of that for only a few more weeks? Plus, I'd be miserably sick the entire time. No, I would not live out the remainder of my life in so much misery that I couldn't even enjoy the love of my family.

I went for the post-surgery MRI and to everyone's surprise, the tumor had only grown ten percent larger. We were happy about that, believing that the holistic treatments were working. Our concern was that we didn't have a lot of time to implement the treatments, or for them to work due to the aggressiveness of the tumor. We were in a race against a relentless enemy, and time wasn't on our side. My friends and I decided to name the tumor Carl, after a character in a popular television show called *The Walking Dead*. It was our way of trying to inject some humor into a grim situation.

During the next couple of weeks, I spent most of my time working the treatment plan. I had so many visitors, phone calls, and texts that I could hardly think. It was a confusing time for me as my eyesight was terrible and my memory wasn't getting any better. I spent a lot of time in Mom's garage, in the makeshift art studio Jimmy had fixed up for me. My art was a refuge. It was an escape from the realities I was facing, into a beautiful world of color and life. Creating art made me feel alive, and I needed as much of that feeling as possible. Even though I was going through the scariest challenge of my life, I recognized how fortunate I was to be surrounded by so much love.

Friends, family, and friends of family, did their best to help. I remember the time one of Mom's friends, Bekki, took me on a mini-adventure to see a jewelry maker, who turned out to be the sister of comedian Ron White. She was just as funny. We had a necklace made, and then I had the sudden urge to buy a salt lamp. Mom was surprised when we walked into her house with three huge salt lamps, and the necklace too, of course. It was such a fun day.

After what seemed like an eternity, Nathan finally returned from the UK. I was so happy to see him, and to have him by my side again. He was an incredible source of peace and calm. Like Mom, Nathan stood by me and supported the choices I was making. There's a lesson there, if you're open to it, and it's one I often talked about with Mom.

The highest form of respect you can show to someone who's battling a serious illness is to honor their choices. You might not agree with their decisions, but dealing with a life-threatening illness is a personal journey. When you stand by someone as they make the hardest decisions of their life, and offer your unwavering support, it will mean more to them than all the advice in the world. That goes for more than just medical advice too.

You may have spiritual beliefs that are important to you, and because you love someone who is facing death, you might have the urge to push your loved one to accept the beliefs you hold dear. Please don't do that. I know it feels like you're helping, but what it really does is increase the stress on your loved one. I lived it and know how it feels. What meant the most to me in my darkest moments, was love. That's it—just love. Love doesn't need to be dressed up, labeled, or confined to one path or system. Love is enough all by itself, because love is all that matters. I think death is a topic that all families should talk about, before they're actually in a situation where a loved one is facing death. Ask yourself what you can do to help, rather than what you can correct, and you will find that love, and acts of love, are the answers.

I was determined to do my best to use my situation to inspire others. My friends and I planned daily social media posts and I was amazed by how many people followed my journey. Increasing numbers of people were offering to help in any way they could. Mom's friends organized a fundraiser, complete with bands, food, silent auctions, and more. We didn't have to do anything because it was all done for us. It was incredible, and I was overtaken with deep gratitude. I wanted to help in some way, and decided to do a painting for the silent auction. I was also working on a large custom piece for a friend at the same time. I tired easily, and painting was difficult with only twenty-five percent of my vision remaining.

I also wanted to record some music I had written, and Nathan found a song that he wanted me to record. There was so much inside of me, so much creativity that had to get out while there was still time. Funny isn't it? How even with death approaching, the desire to create goes on. I think it's how life expresses itself, and it's a way to reveal that dying isn't the end. It's just a change from this to that.

It was early December, and Jimmy came through again. He arranged for me to record some of my songs in a studio owned by one of his friends. Several of my friends traveled from Denver to do the recordings, including Charlie, my cellist, and his wife Erin, who happened to be a photographer. My friend Jen was there too. The recording session was amazing, thanks to the professionals I was working with. It was a dream come true and I grateful.

Not long after that session, my friend Sarah set up another recording session, complete with a band, in a studio in Amarillo. The song I recorded was called "Wings," by Birdy. The session was recorded on video because I wanted to play it at a fundraiser that had been put together for me in Amarillo. It was another way I tried to give something back to everyone who supported me. We recorded the music video on December 7, only a few weeks after my surgery. The fundraiser was being held on December 20. Nathan and I attended it together, but I became so tired that we had to leave early. The fundraiser was a huge success, thanks to Mom's friends and all of their hard work. The crowd was huge and the support immeasurable.

Valerie in the recording studio.

Dozens of people were helping me during those days, and in a variety of ways. I received massages, food, pedicures, prayers, and more. My friends Amanda and Joey brought me boxes of my clothes and personal belongings from my condo in Denver. The outpouring of love was such a beautiful thing to witness and experience.

I felt good most of the time, and tried to continue painting, but it was too much. Art was important to me. It was a vital part of who I was, but my poor vision caused me much frustration and I no longer had the physical endurance for it. I told Mom that I couldn't continue. She took me back into the garage studio and helped me finish the paintings and sign them all. I couldn't even remember how to write my name, so she took me to each painting and guided me through it. She also asked for instructions on what to do with all of my art supplies that were so precious to me. I mentioned that I'd already talked to Josh about it and wanted him to have them. When we finished, she told me that I didn't have to paint anymore if it was too much for me. She comforted me and let me know that I didn't have to do anything I didn't want to do. That was love, and exactly what I needed most in that moment. I never really painted again after that day.

Christmas 2015 was a weird time. Mom helped me get gifts for family and we wrapped them all together. She made everything easy for me. It was a wonderful time spent with family, but with a dark cloud hanging over our heads. I mean, as much as you want to, you can't act like nothing is going on.

Another cloud hanging over my head was Nathan's visitor visa. It was about to expire, which meant that he'd have to leave the country. I didn't want that to happen and neither did he, so we came up with a plan. On January 12,

2016, we quietly slipped away to a Justice of the Peace and got married. We didn't have witnesses or rings. We had each other, and that's all that mattered. A few days later, I received a beautiful necklace from Nathan's mom in Wales. She wanted me to have something to serve in place of a wedding ring. I loved it, and never took it off.

It seemed that things began to move rapidly following our marriage. There was so much going on it was difficult to keep up, but the more challenging life became, the more love was poured upon me. Travis flew back and forth between his home in Wyoming and Texas, just to spend time with me. Jimmy, from the time I was first diagnosed until the very end, made it a point to see me every night before I went to bed. Mom worked tirelessly with a realtor friend in Denver to get my condo sold. She coordinated a moving company to pack up all my stuff and move it to Texas. We put it all into storage that was provided by Mom's cousin Robin.

Jimmy and Nathan would go to the storage place and bring a few boxes at a time to the house. Mom would go through them for me, asking what I wanted to do with everything. One day, we were going through a box of clothes and I said that I didn't care about the clothes. None of it mattered anymore. I asked Mom to give them all to my friends and whomever she wanted. I was holding a Cheeky MaNeeky doll that my friend Jenica had made for me. I held up the doll and said, "Do you know what this is? This is love. Jenica made this out of love."

Isn't the power of love amazing? I had an aggressive brain tumor, my vision was all but gone, as well as my memory. I tired easily and became confused often, but through it all I still knew that love was the only thing that mattered. I had lost so much, but I hadn't lost love. Instead of getting lost in the shadows, it became increasingly clear and present, permeating every facet of my life. It doesn't matter what you have to endure, love is constant.

I became well-acquainted with feeling overwhelmed, along with the constant urge to run away from it all and go to a beach somewhere. My family nixed the beach idea, so Nathan and I decided to go to Mom's cabin in New Mexico. Mom and Jimmy went to the cabin ahead of us to prepare it for our arrival. It was February 2016, and it was cold, but I had to get away even if only for a few days. I felt relieved the moment we arrived. The calm and peace that comes with being surrounded by nature never failed to soothe my troubled soul. I was happy to be there and to have that time with Nathan. All was well for about a week, and then I got a terrible headache. Nothing we did made it better. Nathan called Mom and talked to her about it, and afterwards decided we should return to Texas.

Things started to unravel quickly after that. A few days after we arrived home in Texas, I went for a detox and massage appointment. The intense headache returned. I ended up in the emergency room, and then the ICU. I don't remember much about that time in the hospital, except for what my family told me. Nathan never left my side, and my friend Jenn was there.

Early on, I had told Mom that when things got bad for me, I didn't want people to see me like that. My family honored my wishes and shielded me from too many visitors. The doctors determined that I had experienced a stroke, and I was in and out of consciousness for several days. It appeared that the end of my life was near. The doctors thought it was time for hospice, and my family agreed.

Mom signed the papers for me to go into hospice care. She said it was the hardest thing she'd ever done, but it was according to my wishes. I became unresponsive, slipping into a coma, and the doctors were pretty certain I would die in a short time. By February 25, my breathing had slowed to only four respirations a minute at times. A couple of days later, the doctor told Mom to make funeral arrangements because I wouldn't last much longer.

Well, the doctor underestimated Val Wonder. Mom and Jimmy left the hospital to go make funeral arrangements, and while they were away, I woke up. Everyone was in disbelief, but none more than Mom and Jimmy when they returned to find me sitting up in a chair, talking. I remember talking about islands and going on a trip, and giving everything away.

It was decided that I would return to Mom's house, but would remain in hospice care. I remember having a deep sense of calmness, and asking Mom how I would communicate with her once I was gone. She suggested I come to her in her dreams so we could talk all night. I thought that was a great idea and told her so. My whole life I had vivid dreams and looked forward to sleeping at night. I hadn't dreamt since my brain surgery and I missed it.

I was hopeful to regain the use of my right side again, since the stroke had left it mostly useless. I was content to be with Nathan, my thoughts, my dog, and my family. The first of March was spent with Nathan trying to rehabilitate my right side. He was a physical therapist and had the skill and knowledge to do so. I even tried to paint again, but it didn't work out.

On March 13, Mom and I were alone in the house and seated in her living room. I remember asking her if I was losing my mind. I became easily confused, and my memory was getting worse. She had to remind me that I had a brain tumor, and explain to me again what a tumor was. She even pulled out the MRI and showed me the tumor.

I looked at the MRI image and said, "Oh, I see. Wow, that is big. Is it going to kill me?"

"Yes, it will."

"When?"

"I don't know. A few months probably."

"Oh, okay."

"Well," said Mom, "you don't seem to be upset about that. Before, whenever I explained this, you would get very upset."

"This doesn't upset me, Mom."

"Why not?"

"Because I saw it."

I could see the confusion in Mom's expression. "You saw what?"

"I saw infinity. I saw what it's like after you die."

I told her I had crossed over to the other side and came back while I was in hospice.

"Tell me about it, Val. Tell me what you saw."

"It's not what you think, Mom. This life is tiny compared to infinity." I used my thumb and finger to indicate a half inch."

"You mean eternity?"

"Yes, it's the same thing. None of this is real," I said, tugging on my sweater. "This isn't real compared to that."

"When did you see this? Is this when you told me you saw the beautiful colors?"

"Yes, I saw Gran. She is there. And Grandad. Gran is a front-runner. She is all over it."

"Tell me what you saw, Val."

"It's fluid, it's very pure. It's white and very pure light. The colors are beautiful. It's peaceful and blissful. It's truth, Mom. You just see the truth and everything makes sense. It's this ever-expanding truth. You're happy there. Mom, you will love it. I saw the truth. It's this infinity color spectrum. It's beautiful. It's light that wouldn't stop."

"What do the people look like?"

"There are a lot of them, and they are like fluid and flowing."

"Like a ghost?"

"No, not scary. It's a feeling."

"Who else did you see?"

"Gran was always in the front."

"Are there animals there?"

"I don't know. I didn't see any. This is a tiny fraction of infinity."

"So, you aren't scared to die?"

"No. It's definitely something to look forward to. It's exciting. You're so happy there. It's a good thing and blissful."

"But I will miss you, Val."

"I know, but this is just a tiny time frame compared to infinity. It never ends and it is beautiful. You will be there soon, Mom!"

"I will? When?"

"Well, this is just a very short time—like a snippet of time compared to infinity. You will just go to sleep and cross over. You will go before Jimmy. But that's okay because he has kids and grandkids to take care of him. Mom, you know I manifested Jimmy for you."

"Yes, Val. You told me that last year when I met him."

"I didn't know then that I needed to manifest him to take care of you. But now I am glad, since I will be gone."

From that point on I was ready to cross over. I was at peace with everything and excited about my journey. I had a good talk with my dad, Travis, and other family members. I made sure to tell them everything I needed to say. I was ready, but didn't want to leave Nathan, my friends, or family. Still, I knew from what I had seen that wonderful and exciting things awaited me.

On March 18, Mom, Jimmy, Robin, and Shane headed to Denver for a fundraiser organized by Josh and a few other friends in Colorado, complete with bands, food, and art. I wanted to go, to let everyone know how grateful I was, but I couldn't make such a long trip. All of their hard work wasn't lost on me though, and it was all about love. What more could I ask?

When the family got back from Denver, I asked to talk to Mom alone. I had made a decision and I needed to let her know.

"No more treatments of any kind. I'm not getting the use of my arm, leg, or my vision. I don't want to live like this."

I agreed to take pain medication as needed, and the medication to help with brain swelling, but nothing else. Mom and I sat in the kitchen together for a while, each lost in our own thoughts. We both knew that my decision would escalate my condition, and would probably end my life quickly. Still, Mom and the rest of my family honored my wishes.

It's no small thing when the people who love you most give you the space to make hard decisions about your own life. I know intentions are good when loved ones try to influence such decisions, especially in matters of life and death, but if they knew how much additional stress it brought upon the one they love, they wouldn't do it.

Imagine facing your own death. You know time is short, every unfinished thing in your life will remain forever so, and your mind is filled with unanswered questions. If others began questioning your wishes, warning you about your soul, or expressing their disagreement with your decisions, how would that make you feel?

In the midst of the heaviness, I received some great news. Nathan's mother and sister were flying in from Wales! I was so excited to see them, but I was a little nervous too. I knew my brain wasn't working properly, and my memory was not so good either. I couldn't walk well most days and my right arm was nearly useless. I didn't want them to pity me, or think I was crazy. They're lovely people and, of course, they thought none of those things. They came to see me because they loved Nathan, and they loved me too. I don't remember if I talked much during their visit, but I was so happy they had come. It's no mystery to me why Nathan is the beautiful man he is, because his family is amazing.

By the time the last week of March arrived, my condition had deteriorated quite a bit. I had grown weaker and seemed to be in a perpetual state of confusion. My already short memory became even shorter. I repeatedly asked Mom what was wrong with me, and time after time she would again explain it all to me. I cannot imagine the pain Mom must have experienced, having to explain to me multiple times a day that I was dying of a brain tumor, and each time my reaction being as if it was the first time I had received the news.

Nathan was patient and caring. He cared for me so lovingly, and in a way that allowed me to retain my dignity.

Nathan and Valerie at a fundraiser.

His example was one that I wish for everyone who has a loved one facing death to follow. Love them, but allow them to die with dignity.

I grew too weak to leave my mom's house, and slept nearly all day. Occasionally, I would get up and sit in a chair, but even then I had to have support or I would fall over. Thanks to the wonderful hospice care, I didn't have to endure much pain.

At the beginning of March, I discussed with Mom two things that were important to me. The first was that I wanted her to write the Cheeky MaNeeky books after I was gone. Josh had agreed to do the illustrations. She was a bit shocked, but I told her everything she needed was in my Cheeky binder notebook, where I had made detailed notes about how Cheeky dressed and behaved, and all her adventures. Mom was apprehensive but agreed to try. I explained that I would be with her when she wrote the books, and would tell her what to write. I also talked to her about who I wanted to speak at my memorial service, and that I wanted my ashes sprinkled at Rock Lake, my family's ranch.

It's not easy, talking about your own funeral, but can you imagine being a mother and talking to your child about it? I don't know how Mom did it, but I made sure she knew how I felt.

"Thanks for being my mom."

Her reply beautifully illustrates her loving heart, "No Val, thank you for the honor of being your mom."

On the morning of March 29, I was more alert, and even got to talk to Travis on the phone. Well, I listened more than anything, but it was so good to talk with him. Hearing his voice had a way of waking up the Val Wonder part of me that had been buried inside.

Life can change so quickly. In the fall of 2014, I was making plans to move to the UK. A few months later, I was dying. It all happened in the blink of an eye. I know that some people felt sorry for me, and I get it. If I had a close friend or family member who was suddenly going to die, I would've felt the same way, but in one way I was very fortunate. As tragic as it sounds to die young, I was surrounded by people who loved me. I can't imagine what it would've been like to face death without the intense love that was poured upon me by my family and friends. Being in an atmosphere of love allowed me to make tough decisions and have meaningful conversations with everyone in my life.

On April 4, one month before my thirty-first birthday, I was semi-comatose and couldn't be awakened. Mom began receiving calls and texts from people who said they were seeing me in their dreams. My condition remained unchanged for the next few days. Even though I was unable to respond, my family never ceased telling me how much they loved me. I had always responded well to aromatherapy and Mom diffused lavender, geranium, rose, jasmine, and neroli for me. I loved those scents, and they'd been used for centuries to assist the spirit to detach from the physical plane. Nathan played the sound of ocean waves and the Wholetones Healing Frequency of Music Project. All of those things were comforting to me and were healing tools that I had discussed with Mom. She ensured that the final leg of my journey unfolded exactly how I wished.

A few days later, on Saturday, April 9, I visited Mom in her dreams, just like we planned. I would cross over soon, and I wanted her to know. I came to her on a floating carpet, holding a sign that read 411. When Mom awoke, she tried to figure out what it meant and realized that 4-11 was in two days. She immediately told Nathan and Jimmy about her dream, and that I would pass on the eleventh. Mom came to my room and thanked me for visiting her dreams. She said that it comforted her. Nathan was by my side, caring for me day and night. His love for me was deep, and I never stopped feeling it.

Late on Monday, April 11, I knew I was finally slipping away from my body. Nathan left the room twice that night to get Mom, thinking I was close to death. She would check my heart rate and breathing. Mom repeatedly told me how much they all loved me, how they would miss me, and that it was okay to cross over.

And then it was finished. The suffering, pain, and uncertainty all fell away as I moved toward infinity, just as I had told Mom in her dreams.

You never know how strong you are, until being strong is the only choice you have

Epilogue

*"Do not sway my sweet, sweet soul; do not sway.
Do not find yourself anywhere near the middle."*

Valerie Doshier

There's more to life than what you've imagined. If your conscious experience of life were a movie theater, you'd probably be so absorbed with the movie that you'd forget the person sitting in the chair watching the movie. When you make that subtle shift in awareness, realizing that experiences in life aren't who you are, but rather you are the one witnessing the experiences, everything changes.

When I was diagnosed with terminal brain cancer, I was devastated. It would've been easy to give in to that, to be angry, and rage against the unfairness of it. But the cancer wasn't me, it was an experience, it was the *movie*. I was not the body dying of cancer, nor was I the mind that no longer functioned correctly. I was the one watching it all happen. Make no mistake, I had a few meltdowns in the months following my diagnosis, but in the end, I learned to embrace it all for what it was—an experience.

There's also more to dying than what you've imagined. There are billions of people on planet Earth, and just as many beliefs and experiences. Yet, we will all share the experience of death. You might believe that this understanding would bring us all together, but it doesn't. Most of us avoid thinking about it, much less talking about it. We fill our days and our minds with every conceivable distraction, anything that will keep us from acknowledging the fact that this life isn't forever. The thing is, you can never fully embrace the experience of being alive until you've embraced the reality that death is as much a part of life as being born. It's a circle without end, because life doesn't end, it simply transforms.

So, what's the point? The point isn't how long you live, and it's not about avoiding death. It's what you do in the interim. It's about not being lost somewhere in the middle. The middle is reserved for the mediocre and uncommitted. It's about becoming, expanding, knowing yourself, and actively exploring your potential. Finally, it's about taking all of that and behaving with compassion toward others. Every interaction you have with another is a precious moment, and it's an opportunity for empathy and love. Become who you are meant to be. Live it intentionally, and refuse to be molded by the opinions of others. Be yourself, because there simply isn't enough time to live any other way.

Emerson said, "To be yourself in a world that is constantly trying to make you something else is the greatest accomplishment."

Thirty years didn't seem like enough time to accomplish everything I wanted to do, and it wasn't. But if Emerson was right, and being yourself is the greatest accomplishment one can hope for, then I think I did okay.

If I could leave you with one lingering thought, it would be this:

The only thing that really matters, is love.

Everything else is commentary.

Excerpts from Valerie's Writings

Many of these excerpts are from Valerie's journal, and were written after her diagnosis, with full knowledge of what was happening to her. They offer a glimpse into the beautiful workings of her mind, as well as a light that illuminates a path of genuine love. One of Valerie's most well-known pieces that encapsulated her life philosophy says,

"Do not sway my sweet, sweet soul; do not sway.
Do not find yourself anywhere near the middle."

It became a favorite of many who knew her. Three of her friends had tattoos done with the phrase, "Do Not Sway."

*****

"Cancer. Love.

Technically, I was diagnosed with a stage 4 brain tumor a little over a week ago. I feel I was diagnosed with one of the biggest opportunities of a lifetime for self-actualization."

*****

"Love. It's not what I thought it was. How dare I even think I know what it is now!

Love.

Yes, we know it's greater than us. Yes, it's the highest vibration we can encounter. But do not be mistaken with thinking you know and understand love. That would be hilarious.

Love. It's the only power you need to heal. Everything else is just fascinating and interesting teachings.

Love.
You will never fully reach the end of love, thankfully. I love it. The joke is on you and me.

It is whatever you want it to be.
It is whatever you say it is.
I'm talking about life why I say that, not love.
Love knows what it is and doesn't need us telling it what it is."

*****

"The answer is yours and that is a gift to cherish. I love it. I love how it makes zero sense, but all the sense in the world. I love how mad it makes me, and how much peace it teaches me. I love how scary it makes things feel and love how endless your own bravery can be if you let it. I love how closed in we think this situation is, but really it has provided me more space and freedom than I ever thought possible. I love all of the opinions and thoughts and expectations people latch onto when they learn of this

news. What news? As if I had not had near-death experiences before? We all do, every day.

Whether you like it or not, we all have near-death and near-life experiences every single day. You choose. Death is just as beautiful as life, and I would never be arrogant enough to act like I understand either life or death fully. I love it. I love you. I love every single emotion that comes my way. I am so thankful that I will never stop learning about love, death, and life. It's all the same. I love it. I just got scared and I love it. Now I am smiling because love is taking over everything. I love you."

*****

"Why do people get scared? Why do people cry when they hear about my cancer?

I love you. It is all in your mind, my love. Love yourself with every emotion that comes your way. I love everything! I love how people may think I'm nuts, or genius, or something in between.
(Death is just a different corridor.)
I love how people reading this could be inspired, or may have fallen asleep by now."

*****

"Of course I know that anything is possible, including not getting what I want.

Of course I know I'm not in control of anything, but everything at the same time. It's the space in between.

I do not feel as if I'm getting cancer, but rather embracing it. I'm not afraid of it and would not dream of going through this without embracing every shade of night, every volume of lesson, and every molecule of ugly it has to offer.

I will soak up every ounce of it till it has nothing left to show.

Love. It is the most powerful vibration on Earth and anything is possible once you give it wings. Love conquers all and wins."

*****

"Shed, shed, shed every leaf, till they all fall off. It's all you can do. It's all they can do.

I've lost vision in both my eyes, but my vision can be felt in other places. My music. My voice. My piano. The universe has made it so obvious and I am blessed to see it all so clearly now. I couldn't find the right opening and all my attempts to make sense out of singing or playing piano. I was on the wrong current, the wrong wind stream, the wrong soul line. But there is no wrong, of course. The darkest of dark is still easily seen, as it can't ever be blinding. Listening to your own voice first is the only way to be really heard. Nothing needs to be loud, as a composer breaks all the noise with the very silent tap. A tap more quiet than you would expect.

Alignment is not effort, it is energy, rather. Shed, shed, shed, as it has already left you."

3 Reasons I started
Cheeky MaNeeky

1) I started Cheeky MaNeeky bc she was an authentic part of my creative brain, that needs to be let out for people to enjoy.

2) Cheeky MaNeeky fulfills my heart, spirit, + brain + does the same for others.

3) Cheeky can change the world for the better through her morals, values, + attitude first, then raising a following, then raising money through products to help areas in the world that need it.

a few more

4) to have the freedom of time, money + no constraints geographically

5) to believe in what I started bc the project is worth it

6) to have fun + live authentically

7) to learn massive amounts of knowledge + implement the knowledge ↳ application

Some of Valerie's notes about
Cheeky MaNeeky

"It doesn't matter if my brain cannot write or remember things like I used to. That only aids me to get on with it. Do you agree with the current you're making? Just stop thinking. Perhaps my tumor, my brain cancer, is my saving grace.

Don't stress about thinking, don't stress about the currents. The right energy, the right current, can be strongly mis-interpreted. Stop talking. Only cowards hold on. Less really is more, so stop talking. Look at you trying to triumph the room. Your energy can barely exist in that state."

*****

"True death is your pinnacle. Your truth. Being truly alive is the only way to honor your death.

Do you fear death because you're not sure? Do you fear death because you are too sure? Do you fear death because your thoughts change on it daily? Do you embrace death because you're not afraid to not understand? Do you grip the answers so tightly you forget to give it all away?"

*****

"I can't process my feelings at times, so creating them as something outside of me that I can see helps."

*****

"One of the many things I've learned is there's a big difference between intelligent people and intellects. Just as there is a difference between experience and knowledge.

Sometimes, your brain's memory can't help you and you must dig for your inner wisdom.

My heart never met yours, but can feel yours even still."

*****

"The trick is to never doubt yourself. You will never know your full potential unless you push yourself, so do something that scares you. Drown out any assumptions about your capabilities, and go for it. In your own way, challenge your life. What else are you going to do?"

*****

"Marry yourself first, all day every day, for the rest of your life. The difference in believing and actually committing to these concepts is delicate, fragile, and vastly different. The ocean will cleanse your soul and help you receive the new and release the old. The Earth will provide you abundance and security. The sun will protect you and give you love all over."

*****

"Embrace the journey inside first, and look to nature for advice and guidance."

Music

Valerie's creative spirit knew no bounds, and she expressed it in a number of ways. Besides painting canvases and murals, and creating a children's book character (Cheeky MaNeeky,) she also wrote songs and sang. She was constantly swimming in a flow of creativity and ideas. Often, while going about her daily life, she would use the voice recorder app on her phone to document ideas as they came to her. Unknown to her family, about thirty of those recordings were ideas for songs. Most of them were too raw or fragmented to do much with, but others had potential. Valerie's husband, Nathan, took those recordings to a friend who had ties with Junkyard Studios in South Wales.

The team at the recording studio was able to use Valerie's recordings to create a song entitled, "You Feel Like Home."

The song turned out beautifully, and was released on the first anniversary of Valerie's passing, in 2017. It is available for download on all major online stores, and for listening on all music streaming platforms.

All proceeds from the song go to Nordoff Robbins, a music therapy charity based in the UK. Nordoff Robbins supports thousands of people by working in partnership with a wide range of organizations, including care homes, schools, hospitals, and hospices.

When delivered by a trained practitioner, music therapy can be used to support people living with a wide range of needs. It can help a child with autism to communicate, reduce anxiety for those living with dementia or depression, or provide comfort and celebrate the life of someone facing terminal illness.

You Feel Like Home
by Valerie Doshier

Mmmm Mmmm Mmmm (Intro)
I know it's not true, I know it's not you when I am feeling blue and
I know it's not right, that I've got to fight for you, I just might
I feel in my bones that you feel like home, but I'm all alone
Ah, it's all in my head, it's all in my head, my head.
(Repeated verse)
I thought you would love me, love me
Know you think I'm crazy
Trust me
It'll come back in time
Mmmm Mmmm Mmmm (Outro)

Below is an excerpt from a press release that accompanied the release of Valerie's song:

"VALERIE DOSHIER passed away April 12th, 2016 after a short battle with brain cancer. An aspiring artist, Valerie left behind a plethora of artistic creations, many of which are left unfinished. Valerie believed in the power of love and its ability to inspire others. The same day Valerie was diagnosed with terminal cancer was the same day Valerie said 'If nothing more, I need to be an inspiration to someone.' This track continues Valerie's legacy with nothing but pure motives to inspire and help others.

'You Feel Like Home' is a song that showcases Valerie's creative nature, her projects and moments of inspiration were stored in all corners of her life. The lyrics and vocal to this song were found on Valerie's phone after she had passed. Engaging producers Richard Jackson and Jamie Young based in South Wales and enlisting Grant Tilbury of Trackd Music a social-songwriting-studio app with over 120,000 users worldwide. The team set about putting music to the vocal and song ideas Valerie had laid down on her iPhone whilst going about her daily life in Denver, Colorado. Richard, Jamie, Grant and Valerie's husband Nathan Evans set about discussing her musical influences and creating a song Valerie would have been proud to have released. Valerie's song 'You Feel Like Home' is available to buy from all major online stores and to listen to via all streaming services from April 12th, 2017. All proceeds will be given to Nordoff Robbins a music charity that dates back to 1959 when American composer and pianist Paul Nordoff and special education teacher Clive Robbins developed a new form of collaborative music-making to engage vulnerable and isolated children, which they termed 'therapy in music.'"

Valerie, working on one of her murals.

In Their Own Words

The picture of Valerie's life, and the significant impact she had on the lives of others, would not be complete without hearing from a few people who were closest to her. If this book were a canvas upon which was painted the story of Valerie's life, the insights and experiences of her friends and family are the color that bring it to life.

Nathan Evans, husband

"Val was the feather in the wind, never meant to be contained nor emulated. Just admired.

Val would give all of herself to you in an instant. She had a wonderful ability to love. I know this is something Val worked on every day, to love uninhibited. She used love to guide every action and decision.

She had the type of mind that did special things, saw the world differently, and she was strong, not in a conventional sense but in a way that still has me questioning whether I understand what true strength really is."

Leslie Evans, mother-in-law

"As any mother with an adult son, I watched from afar, physically distanced but emotionally entwined. Privy only to snippets of their life and times together. Intrigued by the young woman who had captured his heart.

I knew from how he spoke of her that she was special, an artist, a free spirit; exquisite and seemingly different from anyone else we knew. Fleeting moments spent in her company that followed provided welcome opportunity for me to witness these traits first-hand.

Valerie captivated our family with her story, one akin to the most tragic fiction. A story in which one of our own was invited by Val's wonderful family to play a central part.

The poignancy and heartache we felt during Val's illness was undiluted by the miles; her life has changed ours. Val lives on in our homes and our hearts; her face in frames on our shelves, her art on our walls. Some people stay with you forever no matter how fleeting the encounter. Val will always be part of our Welsh family."

Travis Doshier, brother

"She was a unique person, there is no doubt. She was very open to new ideas and very genuine in her interest in other people. She really was sincere in getting to know someone and interested in what they had to say. I think this was what drew people to her. She was fair though, in that if you were wrong in your opinion or acting inappropriately, she would

definitely sort you out. I think that is a rare characteristic in today's society. Most people just seem to wait for their turn to speak and push their agenda onto you. Val didn't do that. Sure, she had her opinions and thoughts to share, but she was more interested in yours.

With all the garbage that social media brings, and the social/political platforms that people are able to obtain without really having to earn them through knowledge or experience, it was refreshing to have a person be interested in simply sharing some time and space with you. We need more of that. We need more people that take the world around them for what it is, find the beauty in it, actually care about others, and not expect anything in return, other than being able to share a little bit of life. We also need genuine people that aren't afraid to call out life's problems for what they simply are, and not have an agenda attached. That's who Val was, and that's what made her a strong personality for others to ground themselves to. I try to emulate that in my own life. It's not easy, but I find that seeing how difficult it is makes me appreciate her even more."

Becky Doshier, sister-in-law

"Val has always been a giving person in my life. From the day I met her to when she stayed at our house for a month, she was always so thoughtful and just always wanted to help and share with us anything that she could. She was a great example of a person who could give without expecting anything in return. And it was always from love. She has taught me so much she doesn't even know about.

117

She has modeled how to go though hardships, how to give your heart out without even thinking about it, and how to stand up for the right things. She inspires me to find the true joy and magic in life every day."

Jimmy Boen, stepdad

"Valerie was an unexpected blessing in my life. Since I had raised three daughters of my own, I wanted to meet Valerie after hearing so much about her from her mom. When we met, we had an instant connection. She was always so full of love and fun. I was lucky enough to be able to tell her goodnight every night when she came to live with her mom after her diagnosis.

I learned a lot about living and dying while watching this young lady. I have a picture of her on my dresser and I tell her good morning everyday when I wake up. It just reminds me to appreciate her and what she brought to all of us. It also is a reminder to love and appreciate my own daughters."

Marianne Doshier, stepmom

"One thing I loved about Val was her adventurous side. Me and David went to visit her in Denver and we went to this quaint old bar in Downtown Denver. I told her that as a teenager I wrote a bucket list, one item being to put my toes in every ocean. I told her I didn't realize there was going to be cold oceans. She then came up with a detailed plan, along with her getting help from the bartender, on how to

get me to the Antarctic Ocean, what countries I had to go to, and what time of the year. I loved that side of her. One of my most precious gifts she gave me was a bookmark that she got from a church she visited in Spain. She wrote on it, 'Mama Merv, this was the most beautiful church I have ever seen, you would love it.' Yes Val, it's definitely on my bucket list now. The bookmark stays beside my bedside table in my bible to remind me you can always make your dreams come true."

Hillary Swain Taylor, cousin

"Val was one of those beautiful people who created more than she consumed. Her joy was in creating and her treasures were in experiences and loving people she met along the way. She was unique in that she couldn't be contained by man-made constraints like time, material possessions, or status. More than once, I helped her sell all of her belongings in pursuit of an adventure or new experience. She was happy to leave it all behind and start over wherever she landed. I know that if she were here, she would never claim that she was wise beyond her years. I think she would just tell you that she just never felt comfort in traditional goal posts. She led a brave, real, and gorgeous life—no where near the middle. I miss her more than I can say."

Darla Swain, aunt

"I'll forever remember Valerie for her laughter. When she was very young, she would squeal with delight when she

arrived at her grandparents' house and squeal even louder when she saw her cousins. She continued to laugh all the way through life. During the holidays she would share a story about college and have us all laughing until our sides hurt. I can still hear her giggle through the retelling.

In Proverbs 17:22, the Bible says a cheerful heart is good medicine. Valerie's cheerfulness was a joy for me and the rest of the family. She is dearly missed."

Betty Backer, aunt

"Every morning when I wake, there is Val as my first thought of the day. I sing to her. I often wonder how my young niece can teach me so much. Aren't I the one to be teaching her? I guess not.

When Val lived in Taos, I took her for a hike one fall day. It was picture-perfect weather, with leaves falling all around us. Val extended her arms and danced with the leaves as they fell. Aspen, her dog, tried to catch the leaves. It is one of many memories I will always cherish."

Joshua Finley, friend

"Val,

Thank you. Thank you for all the joy and life lessons, hilarious activities, and adventures. Thank you for caring so much, and for being so real. So Present. Your endless and effortless levity continues to be a beacon of light and laughter.

Thank you.
I miss you.
I love you.

Also: Cheeky Forever! 'It's our world, let's create it.'"

Lindsey Bass, friend

"Val Wonder. Valerina. Val Pal.

We met at eighteen years of age in the dorm at Stephen F. Austin State University. She was a laid-back, no frills kind of girl with a zeal to live life her way. She holds the heavyweight title for her ardent dreams and capricious way of life. Her free spirit and exuberance to be "all things Val" inspired me to color outside the lines of societal and cultural expectations. Throughout the majority of our college years, we shared a home. And as Val would describe it, we shared a room the size of a shoebox.

Our friendship was authentic and unbreakable. While we always had our own unique personalities and aspirations, we were bonded by copious amounts of love, laughter, support, compassion, and shared life experiences through-out our time together. Her daily "Val-isms" always kept my world colorful. She was special. She will be a forever-missing piece to my Earthly puzzle. Her dreams were too big for this earth. I know she is painting the streets of Heaven with joy, laughter, and complete abundance. I will rejoice on the day we meet again. Until then, her legacy and last words to me will be forever imprinted on my soul:

'Do not sway my sweet, sweet soul; do not sway. Do not find yourself anywhere near the middle.'"

Jennifer Marez, friend

"I loved her sense of urgency. It's as though deep inside she knew there was an end in sight because everything was immediate. Panic, but in a good way. Everything was produced quickly and effectively. She painted canvases, murals, then photoshoots, then off to the recording studio, writing lyrics and poems. She never watched TV. Once something was complete, she was moving on to the next. I am the same way. I always thought something was wrong with me, like why couldn't I stick with that one thing. When I met Val, it was a rush of acceptance, like, how amazing are we that we just don't stop at one thing. Let's do it ALL!

She came in my life like a wisp, an immediate friendship. She is still here with me all the time. I feel her. I see her. I dream of her. My life completely improved after we met."

Kristian Daniels, friend

"One of my first childhood friends, that was not my brother or a cousin, was Valerie. I believe that one of the biggest reasons I wanted to be Valerie's friend was because we were opposite in a lot of ways. She was adventurous, and

would jump into anything feet first without considering any type of risk factor.

Val would be the first one to take any dare that developed in our group of friends. If the dare was completed successfully by her, she wanted everyone to share her experience. In these moments, Valerie would insert herself into your decision-making process and become a voice of reason and bravery. That included her describing the experience to you or even offering to complete the dare alongside you so you wouldn't be alone in your feelings of fear and anxiety. She never stopped leading the pack toward adventure. Her bravery was, and still is, infectious."

Katie Hodges, stepsister

"Valerie was my stepsister. Although I only had the pleasure of being around her just a few short times. She touched my heart when I first met her. She had such a beauty and an amazing spirit about her that would brighten up the room the moment she walked in.

She was a person who enjoyed life to the fullest. You knew this by all of the pictures and amazing stories her friends and family told.

I know that she taught me to never take life for granted. You never know when your time is going to come and always live like today is going to be your last. She showed people that life is what you make of it. So make it the best life you can."

Aspen supervising Joshua Finley as he works on the Milburn-Price Culture Museum mural.

Robin & Shane Farris, cousins

"Val was the epitome of courage. When she learned of her diagnosis, I know she experienced extreme sadness along with many other emotions. But the first moment we saw her after her diagnosis, she had a smile on her face and greeted us with love. She even tried to make light of the situation so that we would all feel more comfortable. That was Val, she made everyone feel at ease with her sense of humor, smile, and warm heart.

Once, we were vacationing in NYC one summer while Val was living there. One very hot afternoon, we all decided to head back to the hotel and enjoy the rooftop pool for a while. Val had been with us all day and only had her purse with her. When we arrived at the hotel, Val changed into her swimming suit, which was either under the clothes she was wearing or in her purse. Then after pool time, Val went to our hotel room to shower and get cleaned up. After showering, she came out with her hair and make-up done and was wearing a cute dress and different shoes from the ones she had been wearing all day. Val is the only person I know who can be prepared for anything with just the purse on her shoulder. Amazing!

We loved and admired her for her free spirit. Precious Val, you made the world a kinder place."

Lee Backer, friend

"Val was a wonderer and a free spirit who could fit in anywhere. Her versatility in life was uncanny, yet for those

125

who really knew Val, there was always that underlying unsettledness lurking under her bigger-than-life persona. Val's ability to walk into a room and make everyone around her feel at ease was prevalent no matter what situation she was in. It was almost as if Val had the ability to diminish not only her inhibitions, but the inhibitions of everyone she was around. Her superhuman abilities for love, compassion, and kindness, and to make those around her feel special, were not of this world. She loved everyone, she judged no one, and she brought out the best in anyone she crossed paths with.

Much of what Val's life embodied can be viewed as a lesson in not only how to cope with our current predicament, but in how we can come out the other side as a better human in what will ultimately be a better world. Open-mindedness with understanding that we are all in this together. Selflessness and the ability to make those around you feel better. Genuine concern for the well-being of others. Benevolence in our thoughts and actions. Kindness in our hearts. Generosity in our very soul. Val was the kind of person who you just wanted to be around. At the time you might not have known exactly why, but that desire was always there. Looking back now, I think we all know exactly why. Somehow, Val made you feel special."

Brittany Hill, stepsister

"I met Valerie shortly after she had been given her terminal diagnosis. Although I did not have the pleasure of knowing her all her life, it didn't take long for her soul to impact my life as well as my daughter's life. Valerie was a spectacular

126

artist. She created murals and pictures that will forever be cherished by all who see them. I will never forget this one night that my daughter Keely was watching her paint. They had a sweet conversation, and Valerie told her that they would paint a heart together. Valerie left this earth before they could accomplish this.

Soon after her passing, I had a dream about a heart with wings and knew that Valerie was present. Keely has a kind soul, much like Valerie. When I look at her I think of how loving and genuine Valerie was. I hope to continue teaching Keely to be herself and to become an inspiration to others just like her Aunt Valerie."

Amanda Wilde, friend

"It's hard to understand how a chance encounter over a Craigslist ad can shape your life so much, but it truly did because it brought Valerie into mine. I remember getting off the phone with her that day. We were talking about sub-leasing her apartment in Denver, and Joey (my husband, who also became Valerie's friend) asked me if I already knew her. The conversation was so full and familiar that it felt like we had always known each other. As I got to know her, I understood why.

That smile and laugh. Her silly faces. The adventure and spirit inside of her. The way she always brought me presents for no reason. Our lunch dates. Her creative mind. The wonder and love in her eyes. Her trust in people. How she made instant friends. Her fashion. Her integrity. Her mystery. How she turned into Cheeky after a few cocktails. The nicknames for Aspen. Her undeniable beauty and aloofness. Our shared love of trying new things. This is just a snippet of how Valerie has made my life brighter. Her life and her death continue to guide me to follow my gut and truly remember what life is about. I miss her and I crave time with her again. Valerie, my heart is reaching out to you. Love, Amanda."

Dru Barnes, friend
Spoken at Valerie's memorial service

"It was interesting to witness her love in the world. It's unlike anything I've ever seen, and even now it's like she's still present for me because her light is so bright. Even as I cry, mourning her, she's still so alive in me. She taught me how to live, and ultimately taught me how to die. I've never seen someone meet death with that much courage."

Jennifer Weinheimer, stepsister

"Valerie is my stepsister. Although I didn't know her for long, she made a long-lasting impact on my life. She was a ray of sunshine on a cloudy day. She lived the kind of life that is sought after by many people. She lived her life the way she wanted, and she focused on things that matter. She focused on family, love, and being the best person she could be. She left an imprint on this world with her beautiful art. Her values and views on life are being put into childrens' books to be an inspiration for my son, my students, and

every other person who reads them. She was truly an amazing person.

She is no longer on this earth, but her spirit continues to impact everyone who knew her and even those who didn't. I am blessed to hear stories about her life from her mom, and I continue to challenge myself to be as free-spirited and loving as she was. Live your life to the fullest, don't worry about the small things, and be the best person you can be."

Bekki MaQuey, friend
Spoken at Valerie's memorial service

"One of the reasons why there are so many people here today is because of the special gift that Val had; to make each and every person feel significant. Not just to her, but to the whole planet. She connected with every person she encountered, and had a special way of letting each one know that they rocked the world. Val's spirit was simply bigger than her body. She's in a different form now. Unlimited by the physical and geographical restrictions. I know that her mission will go on."

Tim Spiva, friend
Spoken at Valerie's memorial service

"Valerie was an angel on this earth. She lived and traveled all over the world making friends wherever she went. She had a heart for the homeless and often gave them all the money in her wallet.

[She said to her mom] 'Our job in all of this is to be an inspiration to others.' That's what set Val apart from ordinary. The world is 'all about me.' That's ordinary, but the people that change the world, the ones that draw us closer to them, that make us want to be like them, they put others first and themselves last. Just like Val.

It's easy to see how she touched so many people in so many ways. You could not be around her without feeling her kind spirit and being loved."

Jessica Conn Crawford, friend

"My favorite memory of Val is from when we were very young kids. Sometimes we would go to Val's house after church and we would run around in the fields and get lost for what seemed like hours. We would run and play and jump on hay bales.

Running free without a care in the world."

Andrea Salgado, friend

"So thankful for her heart's imprint on mine. I'll never forget the ways her friendship transformed me.

Val once told me how she appreciated me, which is so her to be fully conscious and thoughtful to say something extraordinarily kind. I remember every detail. We were going down the elevator for a walk and she said, 'You know what makes you so special to me? It's not what you think.

It's not because we share that entrepreneurial spirit and have fun thinking up new crazy business ventures, or because of our random existential life talks, or how we both consider ourselves ladies of true substance but still like to indulge in superficial girly things. It's just how I get to feel in your presence.' She defined it as 'There are no expectations or judgments.' Even at that moment I knew it was simply a reflection of her brilliant light energy.

Val taught me that it's ok to be over-the-top unusual and regular at the same time. Val's passing came very near the time of my son's birth. It's a beautiful reminder as I prepare to have a daughter this year. I think again about how I want to give my children the same gifts Valerie gave me. To love themselves however weirdly awkward or perfectly poignant. Whether she was creating stunning art, or in full goofy Cheeky character, she put it all out there.

One of my favorite memories of Val is coming to watch her band perform at this dive bar in Denver. I had no idea she was into singing. We showed up and she starts belting out this performance with every bit of raw intensity and soul— it was remarkable. My husband turned to me with 'Like what is happening right now?!'

I truly believe she was channeling God. Watching her move through the world not holding anything back is the example I often reference to find inspiration and comfort. I was one of the privileged to experience that light in person, but her spirit lives on through Cheeky's books and every single person who loved her."

Chrissy Voodvard, friend

"We were both living in Breckenridge, Colorado when we met. We met while working at a new restaurant and bar, originally called 7's Restaurant and Bar. It was a gorgeous restaurant, all windows facing the mountain. We took the gondola to work every day. Sometimes we'd see moose, baby moose, and the still beauty of the snow-covered area. What a dream. I'd been a bartender/mixologist for about ten years when we all came together to open this new place. Somehow, Val had convinced the hiring staff that she was a very experienced bartender, which she wasn't.

Upon meeting her, I immediately knew this was one of a handful of soulmates I'd been blessed with. I went out of my way to turn my back to the bar if she got an order for something she didn't know how to make, which was basically anything besides a vodka tonic, a shot, or a beer. We laughed constantly. I slowly began to train her how to make drinks properly.

One day, I came in after her and was impressed to see that she had made about six to seven gallons of pre-batched Bloody Mary mix. I said, 'Well, well, well. Let's give 'em a taste, eh?' That's when I noticed a kitchen-grade amount of cumin sitting alongside the empty cans of tomato juice. I looked at Val and asked, 'Did you put cumin in all of this?' She replied excitedly that in fact she had, because she felt it just 'needed a little something.' I was trying my hardest not to crack up laughing, and instead asked her if she'd tried it yet. She hadn't. So I poured us both a shot glass of her wonder juice and waited. I asked her if she thought it kinda tasted like tacos. She burst out laughing, and I said, "Hey,

133

let's do a special on Bloody Tacos today!' We discretely got rid of all evidence and it remained an inside joke of ours. She taught me not to worry about mistakes. If I'd done what she had, I would have stayed up all night with anxiety that we might be found out.

Val was something to everyone, but she was my best friend. She lived every day the way it presented itself to her, or she created, or both. That was what drew us to each other."

Jenna Choate-James, friend

"Valerie is someone who you cannot forget once meeting her. The way she makes you feel is so special and rare. Her ability to connect with your true inner self is unbelievable.

For Val and I, it was pure goofiness and a complete disregard of anyone around who might be witnessing us speak in the worst English accents ever! Haha. We used to make weird voices and giggle our heads off when we lived together during college. She was up for anything, anytime, anywhere. That's one of my favorite things about her. She is a true badass from the depth of her core.

Our two-bedroom apartment was full of love, chili con queso, and Val's enormous, loving energy—and voice! We also had quiet moments together when we could just switch off and just 'be'.

Our hearts are forever connected and I still think of her every day, whether in dreams or waking life. Till I meet you again. xoxo"

Deborah Sue McDonald, friend and high school teacher

"Valerie (aka Val Wonder) was an edgy little glitter bug that swept her way through our lives, leaving trails of joy, fun, and inspiration everywhere she landed. Her charming, magical qualities drew everyone to her, and entranced us all.

Her stay here may have been brief, but the love she left behind is forever. What better way to head off to infinity and beyond."

Greg & Karen Conn, friends

"We knew Valerie from the time she was born. Our families went to church together and Karen and D'Ann were both pregnant at the same time. Our middle daughter, Jessica, and Valerie were in the same class in school. We didn't see Valerie much after her high school years, until she came to Vega to work on the murals that she and Joshua Finley were painting during the summer of 2014.

That summer, we got to know Valerie as an adult. Young Valerie was still there inside, and it was fun to be around her again. When talking with Valerie, she had a way of soaking up your words as if they were water and she was a sponge. She truly listened to what you were saying and genuinely engaged in conversation in a way that was not typical with most folks. She still had her whimsical way about her, and her artistic side was an amazing thing to watch as well.

135

We tell the stories of Valerie, her murals, and her passing, to visitors from all over the world who visit the Milburn-Price Culture Museum in Vega, Texas. We are the curators of the museum and are honored that our building displays one of Valerie and Joshua's murals."

Deb Hedges, friend

"Val had a spiritual wisdom that was an inspiration in every phase of her life. She was the free spirit we all wish we had enough courage to be, and her adventurous, creative nature is something I aspire to. I still feel her spirit, and see her in all things beautiful.

Val not only touched the heart of those she met, she touched a deep part of their soul. Her journey was, and continues to be, a moving, inspiring, and powerful gift."

Sarah Lookingbill, friend

"Some of my earliest memories as a child included our precious Valerie. She was my oldest friend. We had puffy hair, puffy dresses, freckles, and big glasses. Even from our earliest days of friendship, she was always such a light to be around.

I feel like this doesn't get talked about enough, but the girl was FUNNY! She was always such a character. As we grew older, she never changed. We were always due a good laugh on one of our many phone calls, or holiday visits. I am proud to have known someone who truly lived her life to

136

its fullest. Even if her time in her earthly body wasn't as long as we'd hoped, she was a gift while we had her. Our friendship will always be something I hold dear to my heart. She was my first friend and I'm lucky to have shared so many memories with her."

Wanda Milburn, friend

"When Valerie was painting the historical mural at the Milburn-Price Cultural Museum, she stayed at my place sometimes. Perhaps she liked to be around a person who never had electricity, indoor plumbing, radio, or telephone until she went away to college.

We had an informal relationship that gave us time to relax and talk. We were both busy with our own work, but when we were together, most of our interactions were blurting out thoughts or wonderments that came to us.

It was an unusual time for Valerie. She was back in Vega, Texas, where she grew up, and was seeing her childhood friends, but as adults. She recognized that she was in a transitional time, and was trying to figure out how her innate gift of art could open opportunities for her own health and happiness, as well as benefit her fellow man.

Doing the mural at the museum caused her to think about the people who lived here long ago: the Indigenous peoples, and early traders, and settlers, some of whom were her ancestors who put the first plows in the grassed earth, and fence posts and wire across the land. It caused her to think about the rapid changes in technology and society, even during her own short lifetime.

What other changes would she witness?

In much the same way she approached her art, Valerie tended to think in small increments that she could combine and build on.

I remember when she and her mother came to see me long after the mural was finished. Valerie wanted me to see the attire and hairstyle she had selected for her visit with a new friend in Dallas. She arrived adorned in a yellow suit and yellow high top shoes, and I could see from her manner of speaking and interacting that her time painting the mural in Vega had helped her move into new realms—realms she could use and build her life on."

Patti DeLoach, friend

"Valerie had a magical ability to connect with those she knew on a unique and special wavelength.

For me, it was our mutual love of a favored author. We spoke of this author and his teachings on every occasion we were together. I was always grateful and surprised to hear her thoughts and insights. She asked me my thoughts and would listen carefully.

I would see her with friends and family and the unique connection she had with each one was palpable."

Erika Hamilton, friend

"Val is my oldest friend. My very first friend. Growing up, she taught me a lot. It was the small things that I can truly say helped me to become a confident person. Back diving at the country club pool, driving the truck on the farm, so many things I can remember. She was always ready for an adventure. Even if it was sleeping on the trampoline and howling back at the coyotes. She taught me to find the good in everything. She was one of the wisest souls I've ever known. Not long before she passed, we were texting back and forth and she told me to find something I love in every day, no matter how small, and to appreciate it. I told her that I would do this for her. She wrote me back and said she loved that I was doing it for her, but it was more important to her that I do it for myself. She was/is wise. She lived authentically. I love her and miss her."

Kaylee Gordon Williams, friend

"I met Val years ago when visiting our mutual friend Lindsey. She and Linz were college roommates and she had me laughing the moment we were introduced. Fast-forward a few years and the three of us ended up painting the town of Breckenridge, Colorado together. There, we had so many adventures; hiking, road trips, and concerts—our continued friendship was unbreakable.

One evening, Val and I decided to jump in her car and head to a friend's house for a friendly get-together. We were driving along and all of the sudden, the infamous red and blue police lights came on behind us. OH GREAT!

Val pulled over to the side of the road, rolled down her window, and immediately turned on that charm, with hopes of us getting out of a ticket and on to the party.

The officer was suspicious and asked Val to get out of the vehicle. The other officer, we'll call him Joe, came to my side of the car.

'Mam, this matter doesn't concern you. You can call someone to come and pick you up.'

I looked at Officer Joe like he was insane. 'Sir, not to be disrespectful, but she is my friend. If she goes, I go.'

Officer Joe looked at me like I was insane. 'Suit yourself.'

In the meantime, Val and the other officer were standing at the back of the car. I heard Val, talking to the officer. 'Sir, we have GOT to get out of here! Do you hear that?! There is a BEAR in the woods!'

The cop looked at Val and replied, 'Um, no mam, that is Officer Joe on the other side of the car, talking to your friend.'

A few minutes went by and Val opened my door. 'Okay, get in the back.'

'Oh my God, we are going to JAIL?' I screeched.

'No dude, they are driving us to the party. Get in the back of my car!'

Off we went. Officer Joe followed in the police car and they let us go.

For some reason, I wasn't as shocked as I would've been with any other friend. Because that is just who Val was. Carefree, hilarious, and unpredictable. She had a heart of gold, and the spirit of a wild horse. She had such a beautiful soul and the most unordinary outlook on most things, which is what made her Val.

I could write my own book on just crazy memories that I have with her. She was one of the most amazing people I got to share life with. She will never be forgotten and holds a special place in my heart forever."

Riderless horse ceremony for Valerie.

A Gift of Peace

"I remember when Val and Nathan were visiting D'Ann's cabin in New Mexico. My wife Marianne and I had driven down to Pecos, Texas, on a cattle deal. We were staying overnight in a motel when I had an incredible experience.

It was March 19, 2016, and less than a month before Val would pass. I awoke at five to four. Early mornings were always the worst times for Val. It seemed as though the cancer was more aggressive during the morning hours, compared to the rest of the day. I rarely fall back to sleep after walking up, but that morning I did. I was meditating and praying for Val, and somehow drifted off to sleep. I'm not sure how long I was asleep when it happened, but God sent me a vision.

I saw Val, kneeling and looking off to her left, as a bright light illuminated only her. Everything around her was very dark, but she was glowing like a beacon. Her hair was long again, and her skin was perfect again. She was looking at something amazing, and the look in her eyes radiated peace and hope. She was dressed in a white garment, and glowing intensely from the brilliance that had drawn her gaze.

When I awoke, I was amazed and in awe at what God had just given me. I was finally able to be at peace with the tragic ordeal. God was telling me, 'I have her.'

I shared the vision with Marianne when she woke up, and we talked about it off and on for the rest of the trip. Later, she suggested I share my vision with Randy Friemel, her cousin and a gifted local artist, so we made an appointment with him at his studio. I shared the vision with

143

him and his response was immediate: 'We have to capture that on canvas.'

I was thrilled that he shared my emotions regarding my experience. He had never met Val, so we shared pictures of her. He created an amazing work of art, and perfectly captured my vision.

After Val and Nathan left New Mexico, Val's health quickly deteriorated. I'm grateful that, one day before she passed, I was able to share with her the vision God had given me. By that point, she was unable to speak and was lying on her side when I knelt down beside her. Face-to-face, I told my daughter about my experience. Tears flowed down both our faces, and we shared a peace that will never go away. God had her in his arms and neither of us had to worry any longer.

If I learned nothing else during that time of tribulation, it was that I'm not in control, but God is. 'Be still and know that I am God.'

It took me a long time to share this story, but I felt now was the time."

-David Doshier, Valerie's father

A Love Letter

I wanted to share a few words from my heart and decided to call it a love letter, because my loving relationship with my daughter is what has sustained me. A relationship like ours is pure light. The light is composed of knowing she chose me to be her mom. I've often asked myself, "Why me?"

I think she chose me because she knew I would love her unconditionally, encourage her adventurous spirit, and honor her wishes. After all, it was her journey. I was just honored to be a part of it.

"Mom, you have to write the Cheeky books after I'm gone. I have it all laid out for you in my Cheeky binder notebook."

This was her charge to me. She truly believed I could do it and said she would help me. Each time I sit down to write a Cheeky MaNeeky book, I hear her guiding me in my mind. The ideas, dialog, and images all placed by her. My part in creating the books is merely physical.

Valerie was so selfless that she wanted Cheeky to go on, even after she transitioned. Her vision was to entertain, inspire, and teach a lesson with every book, all done with fun and love. Writing the books has been healing for me. I get to relive the funny things Valerie did as a child, because Cheeky is based on Valerie herself. She was the real-life Cheeky.

Valerie & D'Ann

They say that when you look into someones eyes you see part of yourself looking back. I can only aspire to live and love with the same passion I saw in her eyes. Her bravery, calmness, and confidence going into the next life should touch all of us in the deepest area of our soul. The way she connected with so many people is not of this world.

"Mom, look with your eyes!"

Be present in the moment.
Be adventurous.
Be a gypsy.
See the world.
Love others deeply.
Share yourself.

The love Valerie and Travis had for each other was remarkable. They were amazing together and as individuals. I'm so thankful to be their mother. What an honor. They both insisted that I write a book about my own healing journey. So I did. I wrote, *Autoimmune Saved Me*, before Valerie got sick. It forced me to dig deep and do something I had never done before—write. I'm not sure I would've ever done it without their encouragement. I believe my healing journey helped prepare me to assist Val on the final leg of her journey here on this planet.

"You know Mom, our job in all of this is to be an inspiration to others."

Val did not choose me to micromanage her life. She chose me to teach her how to live her best life. Her best life was all about love. She did it much better than I taught her, and much better than I do. I think of the above quote daily.

It reminds me that it's not all about me, and inspires me to live a life and death of love.

The love Valerie and Nathan shared was inspiring. He showed up in her life at the perfect time, and loved her deeply. I couldn't have taken care of her as well without his help. I am forever grateful. He is the epitome of selflessness and the love of Val's life. He will always be my son-in-law.

Jimmy. What can I say about this man? He came to see Valerie every night before she went to sleep. They talked about traveling and adventure. He even brought a passport application home for her. It laid on the kitchen table for weeks. Every time she saw it she would get excited and plan adventures for him to go on, forgetting that she had seen it the day before. He would hang out with her and give her chocolate when they thought I wasn't watching. Jimmy was my rock.

Every day, many times a day, I think of all the friends and family who supported us. You all will never know what that meant to me. It's a bond that can never be broken.

One more thing. Do you want to help someone who is grieving the loss of a loved one? If so, then talk about their loved one. Don't be afraid to bring it up because you worry that you're causing pain. There's no greater pain than to feel that someone you loved has been forgotten.

When people mention Valerie to me, it makes my day. Knowing that she hasn't been forgotten helps with the ongoing process of healing, and it keeps her legacy alive. My grandkids, nieces, and nephews all know exactly who she was. This is important, and it's a small gift of healing. You can give that gift to others.

I know in my heart that Valerie chose Keith Smith to write this book. It is a book that needs to be read. A chance to inspire and love more deeply. It is a story full of lessons we all need to learn. I am forever grateful to Keith for allowing himself to be an instrument. He was the right one.

It's my hope that you'll read this book, and read it again. It's a small picture of a life that was ruled by one constant—love. In these pages you will find beautiful examples of love, adventure, compassion, and selflessness. You will also find that death is a part of living, and that it can be faced with grace, love, peace, and dignity.

I pray you're inspired, and open your heart to more of all of these things in your own life.

-D'Ann Swain, Valerie's mother

Visions of Valerie

Valerie: *Mom, how will I communicate with you when I'm gone?*

D'Ann: *How about you come to me in my dreams and we can talk all night.*

Valerie: *Good idea, Mom.*

The conversation above took place between Valerie and her mother, soon after Valerie had awakened from a coma and was sent home in the care of hospice. It'd be easy to think that such an exchange was merely to make them both feel better, a way to cope with what they knew was coming. However, the truth goes much deeper.

The matter-of-factness of the brief conversation reflects their incredible bond, as well as their deep-seated belief that life goes on—even after death. They weren't trying to cope, they were intentionally creating a plan to remain connected.

Three days before her transition, Valerie made good on her word and visited her mother in a dream. It would be the first of many such visits.

The following entries are descriptions of those visits in D'Ann's words.

April 8, 2016

"And so it begins.

She came to me on a red magic carpet with a paisley pattern. She was sitting lotus style and wearing a white robe with gold embroidered trim. Her hair was long, her face peaceful as she gazed into the ether.

She was holding an 8x10 gilded picture frame, and in the center of the frame was a painting of thick impasto, kind of smeared down with bright colors. In the center were three numbers: 411

She floated up to me, and then away into the starry night. After I awoke the following morning, I spent some time thinking about the vision. I believed Valerie was telling me when she would pass. In fact, she did pass late in the night on April 11. The official date of death states she passed on April 12, but that was only because we had to wait for a hospice nurse to come to the house and pronounce her death.

I'll always treasure that vision because she wanted me to know when she would pass, and she came to me just as we had talked about days before her death. My friend Patrizia Da Milano painted a beautiful picture of this vision for me. I treasure the painting and it hangs in my home."

April 9, 2016

"I was in the bedroom of a house. The vision was black and white except the gold trim on her robe. I heard a loud shrieking noise. I walked into the hall and looked into the living room. I saw Valerie in the white robe with the gold trim. She had her long dark hair and she was walking/ floating above the floor through the living room to another

hallway. Demons were flying all around her and shrieking and screaming. She walked calmly and steadily and none touched her. As she turned into the bedroom, the demons disappeared and silence fell on the room. I walked through the living room into the other hallway to see where she went. She was sitting peacefully in lotus position on the bed with her back to me.

What did this vision mean? It means she would make the transition peacefully with no spiritual troubles."

April 18, 2016

"One week since her transition. She appeared to me from the waist up. She had on the white robe with the gold trim, long hair. She was smiling and giggling."

May 18, 2016

"I woke up in the morning to remember. She appeared very fluid in the vision that night. White robe with the gold trim. Long hair. Floating above the northwest corner of the garage. Three boxes of Valerie's shoes were still in the garage. My mom was sitting in a chair in front of the boxes, wearing a pink, blue, and white shirt and jeans. Both of them looked peaceful and happy. But why the shoes?

I looked around the garage and couldn't see anything of hers that I hadn't gone through. So I attempted one more time to go through the boxes of shoes to look for the missing green ankle boot. You see, Val's sweet friend, Wanda Milburn from Vega had written me a letter asking me for something of Valerie's to hang on her art/artifact

153

wall in her home. A scarf, hat, something. I had already given most of her possessions away but still had some of her cool shoes. Saturday night, the night before, I looked three times through the boxes for the missing green boot. I knew both had been there before? I was kind of upset because I knew I wanted Wanda to have those boots, but I couldn't find the second one. Since Mom and Val were both around the boxes of shoes I felt compelled to look one more time. Tada! There it was in the bottom of one of the boxes. I had missed it three other times the night before. If I hadn't had the vision I would have never looked in those boxes again. Thanks to my two favorite ladies for your help!"

May 19, 2016

"I was in the water, underwater beside a rowboat. There was debris floating in the water. Valerie was underwater swimming toward me. She had long hair and was wearing the white robe. No one was in distress. What does this mean? It means even though her entire illness was very distressing. She is okay."

July 4, 2016

"We were at our cabin in New Mexico. Valerie appeared to me twice that night. The first time, she was wearing a sleeveless chiffon, orange dress with an empire waist. There was a sash at the waist. The dress was knee-length. She had on brown high heels, and her hair was pulled up into a tight bun.

She said, 'Mom, I have to go with them. I have no choice but I am having fun.'

She was swept away by ten beautiful, flowing, laughing, giggling young women. Val was smiling and excited.

The second vision: I was in the recovery room at the hospital where I work. I was with my boss, Terri Tracy. The room was full of patients and busy nurses. Everyone was smiling and happy. It was a happy place. Terri and I were looking for a new CRNA to help us. I turned to look at the exit double doors. At the right of the doors Valerie appeared. It was just her face.

She said, 'Time is short Mom. Be happy and stay busy. Do happy things.'

I turned to tell Terri to look at her and Terri was gone. Valerie's face slowly faded. She was smiling.

What does this mean? Time is short so make the most of it."

July 17, 2016

"I awoke abruptly at three-thirty in the morning and got up. I was wide awake. I went to the kitchen table and sat down to read. I felt her presence there. Two nights before, my higher self had asked her higher self to let me know what she was doing. Where was she spending most of her time? As I sat down to read I heard beautiful calm ocean waves hitting a shoreline. The same sounds we played for her as she lay comatose before her passing. I got up and looked and listened everywhere, even outside, but they were nowhere except above me in the kitchen. No radio, television, or computer. Nothing was on.

What did this mean? She was telling me that she was spending time at the beach."

September 1, 2016

"Jimmy and I were on our way to our cabin in New Mexico. I had been making an effort to watch the skies closely since her passing. People have told me that the skies have been exceptionally beautiful since her passing. I agree, they have. As we drove I was looking out the window at the clouds. The sky was beautiful. I was looking out the front window to the west and a group of clouds took shape to look like 'I LV U.'

I just stared at them until they went away."

October 12, 2016

"As I've begun to make life changes since Val got sick, I've had some doubts about my decisions. Val was very much a follower of her heart. I tend to be more practical. She told me many times before she passed that she was going to take care of me. She told me that she had manifested Jimmy to take care of me. As Jimmy and I finalized our new business plans, we doubted ourselves sometimes. I told Valerie yesterday (the 6 month anniversary of her crossing) that I know what we are doing is right but I sure could use a confirmation. That night, 10-12-16 in yoga class, we were in a deep meditation. I was very much disengaged from my surroundings and a vision came to me.

I was about to walk through an archway. I looked back and saw Valerie standing with her arms crossed nodding her

156

head as to go on. She had on a cream gauze dress, short-sleeved, above the knee and a thin brown belt. Her hair was long. It was the dress she has on in the picture in Italy as she is walking away as if she is flying. I turned around to look at her again and she waved me on with her hand, as to go on. I walked through the archway and I then became aware that I was in class again. I had tears running down my face and my nose was running.

What does this mean? That was my confirmation."

January 25, 2017

"I have seen and felt Val in others, in sunrises and sunsets, but she hasn't appeared to me in a vision in a few months. Josh came in January to paint the memorial mural of her at the museum in Vega. We all felt her there. Josh told me that the mural was effortless. Patrizia, my friend who painted the 411 vision I had, told me that she felt Val's presence guiding her during the creation of the painting. The painting is moving , mystical, and perfect.

In Yoga class today, during the gong and meditation, I drifted into a higher state. My mom and Val appeared to me in three different pictures. All were flowing and black and white. I will attempt to describe them. I drew pictures of them in my journal. All three of the visions involved me looking up through a round portal. The edges dark and moving. I was in a hole (Earth) looking up at them through the portal and they were watching over me from up above.

#1 A heart with a scepter through it.
#2 Angel with wings fluttering over the portal.

157

#3 Both of them were looking over the edge of the portal down at me. It was all very flowing and peaceful.

What do the three pictures mean? I knew they were telling me that they were close and watching over me."

March 14, 2017

"I was walking on a bridge over the water on a sunny day. Many other people were walking on the bridge. Val walked toward me and was looking at me but didn't say anything. She wasn't smiling but looked beautiful. She had on a white tank top dress with big red flowers on it. Her dress and hair were 1950s style."

March 27, 2017

"Five o'clock in the morning.

I was sleeping and I audibly heard Valerie say, 'Mom' as to get my attention. I woke up startled and looked around. I thought, Val why did you wake me up? Oh well, I was awake and had to get ready. So, since I was up and ready early, I decided to go ahead and leave. Still I was wondering why she woke me up. I backed the car out and down the drive. When I pulled out on the street I realized I had a flat tire. I had just enough time to air up the tire and still not be late. I said, 'Thanks Val for waking me up!'"

August 24, 2017

"I had a vision tonight of Valerie in a long white dress, long hair. She was walking along the halls of the Vega

school, then the Panhandle school, then walking along the dock/harbor in Sydney, Australia in front of the white architectural arched buildings.

Then she was walking along the streets of New Orleans, down on Bourbon Street. She did not look sad or happy— just content to walk and look. Taking her time."

October 2017

"Valerie isn't appearing in my sleep anymore, only during my meditation time. She is looking down at me through a dark hole. Like peering over the edge of a crater. She has flowing hair and clothes, and sometimes wings that look like angel wings. I look forward to seeing her in my meditations."

February 2018

"Valerie is all around me. I can feel her. She tells me to be patient about Cheeky and the books.

She shows up looking at me over the edge of the crater. My mom and Mema are with her sometimes. They float over the top of me and everything is very fluid."

May 2018

"Valerie comes to me telling me that Cheeky is going good and to be patient. Her hair is long and flowing. She has on a translucent white robe. My mom is there but not my Mema."

July 2018

"Valerie and my mom are looking over the edge of the crater at me but are very far away. Very tiny. I ask them to not go away. I still need her help with the Cheeky books. She tells me to be patient."

November 2018

"She has still been far away and tiny in my mediation visions. I was in fear she was going away from my visions but tonight, 11-8-18 she appeared up close again. Lot's of movement this time?"

July 2019

"I continue to see Valerie in my meditations. Sometimes my mom and Mema are there. They are looking down at me over the edge of a crater. Sometimes the hole is very small but always fluid and in motion and in black and white."

Valerie's Art, Music & Cheeky MaNeeky

Valerie's creative spirit was too large to be confined within a single path of expression. Painting, writing, and singing were all methods through which she would share the things that deeply moved her soul. You can experience some of this for yourself by exploring the information below.

Music

"You Feel Like Home" is an original song that was discovered on Valerie's phone voice recorder. The song is available for purchase and download on iTunes, Amazon Music, and other major online stores, and to listen to via all music streaming services. Proceeds from all sales will be given to the Nordoff Robbins music charity.

Art

Valerie's amazing artwork can be viewed and purchased on the **cheekymaneeky.com** website. Visit the site, find the pieces you would like to purchase, and send D'Ann Swain a message via the website. You can also find Cheeky MaNeeky on Instagram and Facebook.

On **cheekymaneeky.com**, you'll also find the Cheeky MaNeeky book series, coloring books, T-shirts, stickers, and more! Money from all sales is used to keep Valerie's vision for Cheeky alive for future generations.

Note: As of the time of this writing, you can search the following words on YouTube and discover even more about Valerie Doshier.

- A Tribute to Val Wonder
- Val's Memorial Service
- Valerie Doshier Ashes Tribute
- You Feel Like Home
- Wings, sung by Valerie Doshier

Acknowledgments

This book took on a life of its own. From the time it was decided Valerie's story would be written and the time it was finally completed, the book transformed many times. Keith and D'Ann put in hundreds of hours of work, shared countless emails, phone calls, and text messages in order to make this book a reality. However, without the help of many other people it would have been next to impossible to complete.

Keith would like to thank and recognize the following people:

D'Ann Swain, for your relentless efforts to ensure Valerie's story would be told. You relived every precious moment of your daughter's life, including the most painful of memories. With all of my heart, thank you.

David Doshier, for the honor of writing about your daughter's life. Thank you for working with a fellow father so that the world could benefit from Valerie's wisdom and passion for life. The way in which she lived, and faced death, will influence many people for good.

Greg and Karen Conn, for being my first friends in Vega, Texas. You took me under your wings from the very beginning and I'll be forever grateful to you both. Without your kindness, generosity, connections, and open hearts this book may have never been written. I cannot thank you enough.

165

My daughters, Jennifer, Lindsey, and Laura, for answering my endless stream of questions and requests for feedback. Your wisdom and insights were instrumental in improving the quality of this work.

Deborah Sue Glass McDonald, for your kindness, encouragement, and boundless generosity. Thank you for giving me a stress-free place to stay as I finished the book. Also, thank you for the wonderful conversations, sharing your food, and mostly your passion for living. You're such a bright light in this world.

Valerie's husband, Nathan Evans, for your heart toward this work. Your contributions, will be felt in thousands of other hearts around the world. Thank you.

Thank you to all of my beta readers. Your critique and input was invaluable to this work, and I'm grateful to each of you for taking the time to read it and offering your thoughts and insights.

Sylvia Marusyk
Cary Wyninger
Deborah Sue McDonald
Lynda Cunningham
Karen Fangman
Lindsey Behee
Anna Timperley

Davina Haisell, for generously offering to apply your skills as a professional editor and proofreader to this book. Your creativity and expertise are unmatched. I don't know what we would've done without you. Thank you for being a part of our team and helping to make this work the best it could be.

Lastly, I want to thank the wonderful people of Vega, Texas for welcoming me with open arms. Your kindness and hospitality contributed to my rich experience of writing this book.

D'Ann would like to thank Keith Smith, for having an open heart and mind. He has treated this entire project with so much reverence and respect. I know in my heart that Val chose him. She chose well.

I am forever grateful to our friends and family that have contributed to this book. I appreciate your time and love for Val. It warms my heart to know that so many of you feel so passionate about telling her story. Piecing the timeline together was no easy task. I think we got it right, but we couldn't have done it without the help of those who were in her life. The lessons to be learned from her journey are too numerous to count. I still learn something from her every day.

I'd like to express my gratitude to Erin Nutini and Jennifer Marez, two amazing photographers whose pictures appear throughout this book.

I am thankful and humbled to have been a part of this project, and most of all I'm honored to be Valerie's mom.

Keith E. Smith

About Keith

Keith E. Smith is a nomad writer traveling around the United States, and is the author of five books, including:

- *Black Chamber: Paradise Lost* - action thriller.
- *Your Time is Now* - inspirational self-help.
- *Night Words* - A book of poetry and prose.
- *The Top Ten: Lessons for Successful Business Leaders and Managers* - coauthored with Mandy Clark.

Keith has also been a ghostwriter for more than five years and began blogging in 2010 on his website **StraightUpLiving.com**

D'Ann Swain

About D'Ann

D'Ann Swain is a registered nurse with more than thirty-five years of experience in the medical field. She's also the author of the *Cheeky MaNeeky* book series as well as *Autoimmune Saved Me!: A Holistic Roadmap for Healing & Restoration.*

After suffering from autoimmune disease and not experiencing any sustainable relief with her treatments, she set her intentions to restore her health holistically, and it worked.

Visit her online at **swainholisticsolutions.com**

Made in the USA
Columbia, SC
24 February 2021